Food for Life

TRANSITIONAL RECIPES FOR
FOOD COMBINING AND BLOOD TYPING

U. B. RIGHT

– *First Edition* –

Food for Life: Transitional Recipes for Food Combining and Blood Typing
U. B. Right
Copyright © 2005 by Royall World Productions
Published by Royall World Productions
1608 North 13th Street, Kansas City, Kansas 66102
800.331.7668
ISBN: 0-9768115-0-2

Introduction

This cookbook is the first installment in a transition to food-combined, blood type-indicated recipes, and to food facts that will assist in eating to live. The recipes are all cane sugar, bovine dairy, salt- and wheat-free, and completely health conscious. With the exception of salmon, because of its exceptional health benefits, and goat cheese because of its alkaline reaction in the body, this cookbook is a compilation of a new and interesting way of cooking.

The recipes are unique in that they are all formulated to be healthy and at the same time efficient. For instance, with the Apple Peel Tea Recipe you are instructed on how to use all of the apple except for the core. There are also innovative recipes on using carrot and fruit pulp from juicing.

Foreword

By Marvin Macintosh, M.D., M.P.H.
Director of the Community House of Wellness, Kansas City, Kansas

I have had the opportunity to review numerous recipes and recipe books; the *Transitional Recipes for Food Combining and Blood Typing* is a new and exciting level of thinking when it comes to eating properly. Eating right, combining foods and/or ingredients properly and eating according to personal blood type are all ideas one usually does not consider when compiling a book like this.

As I reviewed the recipes, I noticed that all of the recipes are choices that persons with any health conditions can enjoy without fear of their condition being made worse. In fact, utilizing these recipes are enjoyable as well as "health promoting." All have minimal amounts of sodium, sugar, and cholesterol-laden fats. People with hypertension, diabetes, thyroid disease, arthritis, cancer and obesity can indulge knowing that what they are eating will actually help to reduce their disease burden.

These recipes are calorie balanced, meaning the amount of calories from protein, carbohydrates and fats are in favor of promoting health. No more calorie counting needed when using the recipes contained within this book. These recipes fit any and all dietary constraints.

Eat and enjoy! Watch your weight and reach the level your body habitus is supposed to have! Food is medicine and medicine is food.

Eating is such a pleasurable experience. It is a social event. It is a mechanism for establishing relationships in all walks of life. Marriages are decided, alliances are made, businesses are established, friendships are discovered—eating is more than replenishing the fuel source for our bodies to function.

However, we cannot lose sight of the fact that eating properly is what we must strive to do. Eating can allow for maintaining good health, or can allow illnesses to overtake us. Science has shown that a very large percentage of the illnesses that occur are the result of what we eat. Obesity, cancer, arthritis, heart disease, hypertension, and diabetes are all occurring in epidemic proportions and they are either caused by or affected by what we eat. As elementary as it sounds we should not be living to eat; we must learn how to eat to live.

Foreword (Continued)

You truly are what you eat. Our bodies require certain substances in order to function properly. Except for the energy from the sun being absorbed through our skin, all substances go through our mouths. A balanced intake of water, protein, carbohydrates, vitamins, minerals, fats and fiber is what we need for maintaining normal internal processes so that our bodies will live disease-free for a very long time. Consider the following principles:

1) **Our bodies are 70 percent water.** We cannot live very long without this vital nutrient. It is a cleanser, a lubricant, a vehicle for removing toxins, a vital element for chemical reactions, and an essential component of every system. Our bodies are like very sophisticated chemical plants—using, producing, storing and eliminating chemicals; therefore, nothing occurs in our bodies without the use of water. Drinking 8-10 eight-ounce glasses of water per day will keep many illnesses away.

2) **Dieting is not what we are to do;** eating a well-balanced meal is what is required. Nutritious meals should be composed of fresh fruits and vegetables, whole grains, very little fats and sugar. We must minimize or eliminate processed foods, refined sugar and saturated fats. Science has proven that all red meats should be stricken from our diets. We should eat fish instead, especially the cold water fish.

3) **Eating the right foods is the first step.** Secondly, eating the right quantity and at the right time is next. Keep your portions such that you have a total caloric intake between 1800 and 2200 calories per day. It may take a little investigative work initially to remember what quantity of food will provide this level; however, after a while it will be automatic. Divide your meals such that your main meal occurs midday (not late evening). This will allow for proper digestion to take place.

4) **To achieve the most efficient state of proper eating**, in addition to the above, combining foods properly and eating according to your blood type is vitally important. Some foods, when eaten together, cause intestinal ailments, like gas, bloating, constipation, diarrhea, allergic reactions etc. Some foods act like slow poisons because they are not compatible with your blood type.

5) **Lastly, the intake of food supplements should be done using "common sense"** discretion. Food supplements are exactly what they are labeled—supplements. They are not to take the place of our food, but rather, augment our food. Sometimes the food we have available cannot provide everything we need. In many areas, the farmland has been depleted of many nutrients, therefore supplements are needed.

There are many other ideas that can be expressed about eating; however, this book is designed to stimulate your wanting to seek additional information. Learning how to eat to live can be fun—and the benefits are immeasurable!

Food Is Medicine

The food you eat can be the most powerful form of medicine or the slowest form of poison. Food affects the body more slowly than drugs; however, it is a much safer and more efficient antidote. Food works by removing the cause of illness, whereas drugs merely relieve the symptoms.

The body will heal itself if given the proper nourishment, rest and exercise. Every second you are alive, messages are being sent from head to toe to restore balance in the body. Proper use of food is critical to maintaining this balance.

The purpose of eating is to nourish the human body, not to cater to its (the material's) appetites. It is true: You are what you eat—you physically and mentally are what you eat and think. The food you eat as well as the combinations of food can make for disturbances or disease in your body. Even when their diet is wholesome and nutritious, many experience digestive problems and other discomforts. The solution: "food combining."

Food combining is putting certain foods together for optimal digestive results, eliminating digestive disruptions, and the inability to receive nutritional value. Even in consuming a great deal of food, if you don't receive the proper nutrition, is a waste of food and energy. It tends to clog the intestines needlessly, overburdens the liver and potentially causes some degree of acid in bodily tissue. If you continuously eat large quantities of food in this way, it invites various deficiency conditions that effect your overall health. Large quantities of starches and proteins consumed together, or combining alkaline-reacting fruits with starches, can create disturbances in the balance of the body.

One of the most serious disturbances in this balance is in the body's elimination system. Faulty eliminations are at the root of nearly every disease. Constipation or even incomplete evacuations can allow for the re-absorption of poisons, which in a normal state would be filtered out of the body. Occasional cleaning of the intestines by colonic irrigation and the periodic use of laxative foods in the diet will bring about better conditions for elimination. Examples of effective laxative foods include prunes and figs. Avoid sticky or gooey foods and/or foods that will become sticky or gooey when mixed with digestive juices (such as flour and water makes glue, soft donuts make stomach cement, etc). Because these foods will adhere to the walls of the colon, they will cause a variety of disturbances, including gas, indigestion, poisoning and more.

Food Is Medicine (Continued)

Also, these types of foods are mucus and acid forming. Additionally, be sure to include the daily required amount of drinking water in your elimination plan.

Lack of water in the body produces a burden on elimination systems that are normally cleansed through the colon, causing a backup into the capillary system. Drink 1/2 your body weight in ounces each day. For example: 150 lbs. = 75 oz. of water a day. The process of digestion also requires high temperatures, so be mindful that consuming cold water while eating stops the process before the food has fully digested. Drinking plenty of water at least 40 minutes before food enters the stomach allows digestion to work properly, thereby alleviating skin problems and correcting eliminations from the body. All channels of elimination must be kept in equilibrium, so as not to overtax the lungs, liver, or respiratory system.

Digestion requires a great deal of energy so allow the body to rest occasionally. Fasting is an effective method for allowing the body to rest from digestion and it gives the body the needed energy to heal. Fast three days at the end of each month.

Once the body has rested, further cleanse the body with laxative foods and fruits. Then, build the body with fresh vegetables and vegetable juices. We are building the houses in which our entities live. We all can choose whether to live imprisoned in dilapidated housing or free in a beautiful villa.

Human beings take in the vibrations and influences of food and the circumstances surrounding its preparation, so eat the food of a cook who is at peace. Eat only when you are at peace so your body may best utilize the energy and influences being consumed. Eat slowly, chew thoroughly and make meals as relaxed as possible. When you eat quickly you swallow larger lumps, which enter the intestine undigested.

Another important aspect of the idea of food as medicine is eating by blood type. Blood typing is the science and investigation of the strengths and weaknesses of each blood group. Research shows that the digestive and immune systems are most affected by the food we eat. This knowledge allows us significant opportunity to improve our challenges or weaknesses through the right eating habits. Blood typing helps us further define which foods are medicines.

Food Is Medicine (Continued)

Large amounts of lettuce should be eaten by everyone. Lettuce destroys negative influences in the blood. Fried foods should be avoided; vegetables will build brain matter faster than sugars and meats. When our bodies are alkaline with things like lettuce, carrots and celery, the blood supply will maintain a condition for immunization against contagious diseases.

All fruits have an alkaline ash. Food is determined to be alkaline or acid by comparing the residue ash from digestion. When food contains more alkaline than acid minerals (when the minerals calcium, magnesium, potassium and sodium dominate over chlorine, nitrogen, sulfur and phosphorus) it will be classed as alkaline. All grains with the exception of millet have an acid ash. Wheat and oats are the most acidic. Fruits and vegetables contain citric acid, malic and other acids, they have an acid ph reaction in digestion, but because of the high content of alkaline-forming minerals, their reaction is always alkaline in the bloodstream. This helps to neutralize the waste products of metabolism which are always acidic. Most toxins in the blood stream have an acid reaction that eventually neutralizes the alkalinity in the blood.

Approximately every seven years the body renews itself. Each cell of the body becomes new. If your body is clean, the material the cells use to rejuvenate will be clean. If not, your body will use the decay and debris to build your body, accelerating the aging process. Eating in a precise and detailed manner allows us to pay attention to what we will physically become from what we consume now. It also allows us to determine what our children will become physically once conceived.

A beautiful body is the result of perfect health. What you eat must be taken seriously and your eliminations must be balanced throughout the systems of the body. Place in your mind how you want to be physically and you will always be elevated in that direction and settle for no less. A system has already been put in place for our success.

Once we master our appetites, the battle is won.
We strengthen our WILL and WILL makes more WILL.

"For the body is indeed the Temple of the Living God."

How does food combining relate to blood typing?

Food combining is based on the fact that each type of food requires different lengths of time, different enzymes, and different pH balances (the degree of acidity or alkalinity of the digestive juices) for proper digestion. Some foods, like proteins, require an acidic environment. Other foods, such as starches, break down more easily in an alkaline environment. Combining foods that require different digestive environments causes indigestion (gas, constipation, diarrhea, nausea, bloating, fatigue) and results in incomplete digestion.

Incomplete digestion forces the body to spend energy creating more digestive enzymes (and even white blood cells), thereby robbing it of the energy it needs to create tissue-building, metabolic enzymes.

The following are three main guidelines when transitioning into food combining: for optimal digestion avoid combining proteins and starches, and avoid combining fruits and vegetables (however, you can use lemons or lemon juice freely, as they go well with all food, act as preservatives and have therapeutic benefits).

Now, how does food combining relate to blood typing? In the past, the mainstream medical community remained largely unaware of the breakthroughs linking blood group individuality to diet and disease. In recent years, there have been thousands of reports, published from individuals of every blood type, based on the level of improvement they experienced in diseases and chronic conditions after using the blood type diet plans. Many of these results are fortified by hard data, including blood tests and physician reports. Most reported astounding improvements in digestion, an overall sense of energy and well-being, and weight loss. The significance of these findings goes beyond a simple degree of satisfaction or a beneficial health improvement; it scientifically challenges the validity of any "one size fits all" diet philosophy.

The ABO blood groups are an important key to the body's immune system. They control the influence of viruses, bacteria, infections, chemicals, stress, and the entire

How does food combining
relate to blood typing? (continued)

assortment of invaders and conditions capable of causing disease and weakening immunity. Through their unique antigens they accomplish this by serving as biological gatekeepers.

Antigens are chemical markers, typically proteins, found on the cells of our bodies and on most other living things. Any foods that are ingested may become antigens depending on a person's blood type. Based on this fact, foods that are neutral for a blood group are "food for the body" (meaning that they maintain the body). Foods that are beneficial for a blood group are "medicine to the body" (meaning that they actually strengthen the body). Foods that should be avoided by a particular blood group are "toxins to the body" (meaning they weaken the entire system). Blood reference guides included in the back of this book will allow you to make the most mathematical decisions regarding food selection for your blood group. "One man's food is another man's poison."

Table of Contents

Table of Contents (Continued)

Almonds

Almond Fact Sheet

Neutral for all blood types, almonds are rich in essential fatty acids, protein, minerals, and vitamins E and B complex.

- Almonds are compatible with all other protein foods; however, they do not mix well with starch. The ideal way to eat almonds is to eat them on their own or in combination with other vegetables and salads. Any difficulty with digestion that is experienced may be due to improper food combining rather than the nut itself.

- Almonds are high in fat, and the majority of it is the healthy unsaturated type.

Kitchen Tips

- Keep raw or shelled almonds refrigerated or frozen to prevent rancidity because of their high fat content.

Scanty Breast Milk Mixture

- If breast milk is scanty, try this mixture of almond milk and herbs:
  Place 10 shelled almonds in water overnight. Then peel them, put them in the blender, add a cup of hot water and puree them. Pour almond milk into a glass and add a pinch of ginger powder, cardamom and saffron. Also add a teaspoon of date sugar. Drink this mixture twice a day, in the morning and in the evening. This will help strengthen the quality and the quantity of the breast milk. This also assists in battling fatigue that comes with or after illness.

- NOTE: if you are making almond milk to assist with easier digestion, blanch, peel and strain through a very fine strainer or cheese cloth. After straining, the pulp can be used in crackers and other dishes.

- Almonds are proteins—digestion time is approximately 4 hours.

- Soaked proteins combine best with other foods and are more easily assimilated by the body than nuts that have not been soaked or sprouted.

- Raw almond butter—a great alternative to peanut butter.

Almond Butter Recipe

INGREDIENTS:

1 lb almonds

3 T maple syrup (or sweeten to taste)

1/2 cup olive oil

DIRECTIONS:

Roast almonds and then soak them overnight (for every 1 cup of almonds, soak in 2 cups of water). Put roasted, soaked almonds in blender, then pour olive oil and maple syrup in a little at a time until mixture is smooth.

BLOOD TYPE GROUPS:
A B
AB O

Almond Ice Cream Recipe

INGREDIENTS:

1 lb almonds

1/2 cup apple pectin (see Apple Peel Tea Recipe, page 17)

6–10 dates

DIRECTIONS:

Soak almonds and dates in separate containers overnight. Water should be two inches above the almonds. Water should just cover dates. Blend almonds and strain through a cheese cloth. Repeat several times until milky-looking color disappears. Combine apple peel pectin, dates and almond milk in a blender and blend thoroughly. Freeze 3-4 hours.

To make a warm drink, add 1 teaspoon per cup to saucepan with almond milk and heat.

BLOOD TYPE GROUPS:
A B
AB O

Almond Milk Recipe

INGREDIENTS:

1 lb almonds

1/2 cup water

DIRECTIONS:

Soak almonds overnight in separate containers. Water should be 2 inches above the almonds. Blend almonds and strain through cheese cloth. Repeat several times until milky color disappears.

To make a warm drink, add 1 teaspoon per cup to saucepan with almond milk and heat.

BLOOD TYPE GROUPS: A B AB O

Maple Almonds Recipe

INGREDIENTS:

4 cups almonds

3/4 cup maple crystals

3 T maple syrup

2 T olive oil

DIRECTIONS:

On a cookie sheet, place the almonds in a single layer and bake at 300° for 15 minutes. Heat skillet on medium high and add maple crystals. Add the freshly baked almonds and stir in olive oil. As the maple crystals begin to melt, add maple syrup and mix thoroughly. Pour almond mixture onto a sheet of wax paper. Spread into a single layer to cool.

BLOOD TYPE GROUPS: A B AB O

Apples

Apple Fact Sheet

Compatible for all blood groups, apples are crisp, white-fleshed fruits with red, yellow or green skin. They range in taste—from moderately sweet and refreshing to pleasantly tart—depending on the variety. The apple is a member of the rose family, with a compartmentalized core which classifies it as a pome fruit.

Nutritional Data

- Apples are a healthy, no fat, cholesterol-free, fresh dessert, as well as an excellent source of fiber. An average-sized apple has 5 grams of fiber, which supplies 20 percent of the daily fiber recommendation. Apples are also a natural source of vitamins A, B1, B2, C, niacin, and minerals calcium, phosphorus, iron, iodine and potassium. Recent studies suggest that naturally-occurring compounds called flavonoids may reduce the risk of heart disease and inhibit the development of certain cancers. Dietary fiber and pectin, a fiber component, are found in apples. Some researchers believe fiber and pectin aid digestion and may also help limit the absorption of cholesterol in the body.

Therapeutic Benefits

- Apples' two types of fiber pack a double punch that can knock down cholesterol levels, reducing your risk of hardening of the arteries, heart attack and stroke. Apples' insoluble fiber works like bran, latching on to LDL cholesterol in the digestive tract and removing it from the body, while apples' soluble fiber pectin reduces the amount of LDL cholesterol produced in the liver. Eating two large apples a day has lowered cholesterol levels by up to 16 percent! When it comes to bowel regularity, the two types of fiber tackle the job—no matter what it is. Both the insoluble fiber in apples and the soluble fiber in apple pectin help relieve constipation, helping to prevent diverticulosis. The insoluble fiber works like roughage, while the pectin, which is found primarily in the skin, acts as a stool softener by drawing water into the stool and increasing stool bulk. On the other hand, because pectin firms up an excessively loose stool, it is also used to treat diarrhea.

At the Market

- Look for apples that are firm, fragrant and free of bruises. Store apples in the refrigerator; they do not last as long at room temperature. To keep apples for a long time, place them in a plastic bag and spray them with a mister once a week and they will last 4 to 6 weeks, depending on the variety.

Kitchen Tips

- Red Delicious® are considered to be good eaten raw or on a salad. Once you cut the apples, toss the pieces into lemon water to maintain original coloring.

Apple Peel Tea Recipe

INGREDIENTS:

10 apples

Makes 4 servings of apple sauce

Makes 8-6 oz. glasses Apple Peel Tea

DIRECTIONS:

Apple tea is a wonderful beverage that is simple to make. When juicing apples, peel and core the apples first. Doing this will allow you to produce three food items from one: apple juice, apple sauce from the pulp, and apple peel tea. Peel apples and place the peels in a glass or stainless steel pot. Cover with water and bring to a boil, then simmer for 15 minutes. Strain into mugs and sweeten, then squeeze a lemon wedge into the cup. You can refill the pot with water (many times) to make more tea, until the peels begin to break up. Once this takes place, blend the peels to make apple pectin, which can be used for making almond ice cream and lemon pudding, and to make fruit rollups pliable. To make apple sauce combine the apple pulp with 1/4 cup of the apple juice, sweeten with dates and heat in sauce pan.

Makes 4, 8 oz. glasses

BLOOD TYPE GROUPS:
A B
AB O

Transitional Recipes for Food Combining & Blood Typing

Raw Food Cookies Recipe

INGREDIENTS:

3 apples

1 1/2 lbs. almonds

6-8 dates

DIRECTIONS:

Soak dates overnight by covering them with water. In a food processor, grind 1 lb of almonds into coarse almond flour. Grind remaining almonds into coarsely chopped almonds. Peel, core and dice apples. Combine all the ingredients in a food processor and process into paste. If paste is too dry, add a portion of the water from the soaked dates. Pat out into desired-sized cookies and dehydrate in an oven on warm or lowest setting (overnight) or until cookies are at desired firmness.

BLOOD TYPE GROUPS:
A B
AB O

Transitional Recipes for Food Combining & Blood Typing

Fruit Roll-ups Recipe

Fruit Roll-ups are an excellent treat that can be made with pulp that is left over after juicing.

Stretch plastic wrap over a baking dish and spread pulp over dish, making a thin layer of about 1/8 - 1/4 inch. Place the baking dish in the oven and set the oven setting to warm for 6-8 hours or until dry. The roll is easily removed from the plastic wrap for cutting into shapes. Or you can leave the plastic wrap on and use cooking shears to cut strips and then roll up and wrap.

Apples and pears contain lots of pectin and can be dehydrated as is with grape, pineapple, strawberry, blueberry and other fruit pulps. Blending apple (or pear) peels with apple (or pear) pulp will cause roll-ups to be pliable rather than crispy.

BLOOD TYPE GROUPS:
A B
AB 0

Apple Pear Sauce Recipe

INGREDIENTS:

1 large apple peeled and cut into chunks

Large pear peeled and cut into chunks

1/2 cup pitted prunes, soaked overnight in 1 cup of spring or filtered water

1 dash apple sauce spice

1 cup apple juice

DIRECTIONS:

Blend fruit and apple sauce spice at medium speed in a blender; add fruit-soaked water and apple juice until sauce is thick. Serve with apple-pear breakfast treat.

BLOOD TYPE GROUPS:
A B
AB 0

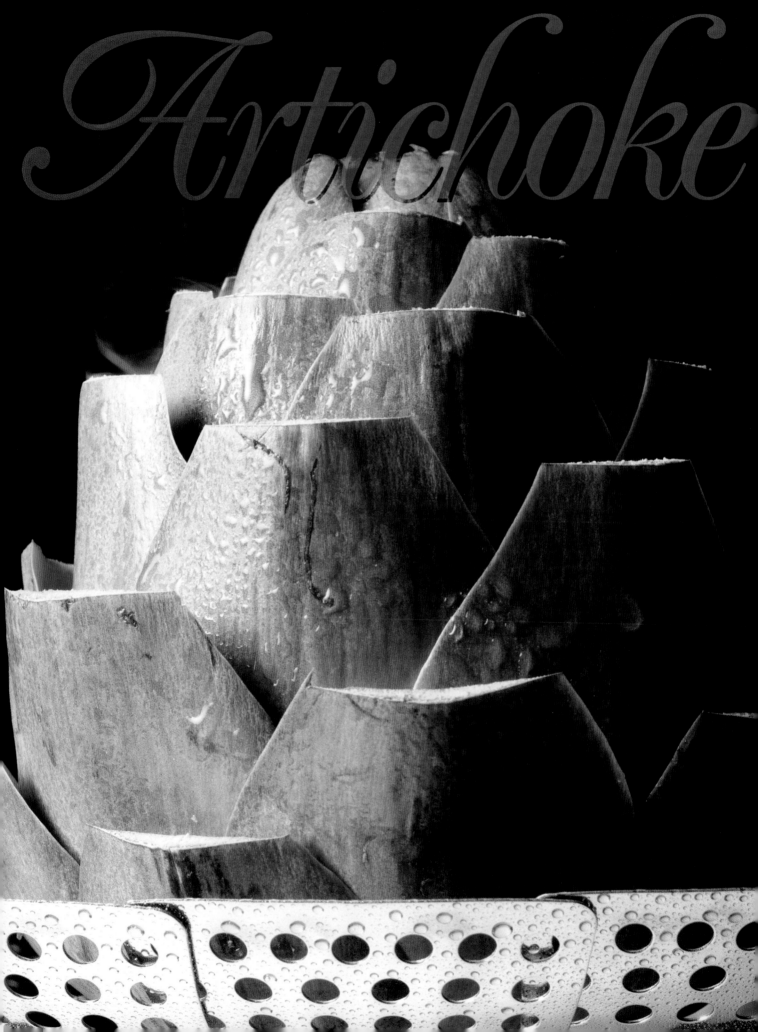

Artichoke

Artichoke Fact Sheet

- Beneficial for blood groups A and O (and should be avoided by B and AB blood groups), artichokes are a part of the lettuce family. Globe artichokes are good sources of potassium and folate. Cynarin, found in the edible base of globe artichoke leaves, may improve liver function. Artichokes combine with protein and starch. The average artichoke contains 80 milligrams of naturally-occurring sodium and approximately 53 calories.

Nutritional Data

- Artichokes contain small but significant amounts of calcium, iron, phosphorus, niacin and vitamin C. Artichokes also contain magnesium and potassium, which are good sources of minerals. Artichokes are fat-free.

Therapeutic Benefits

- Research studies in Germany have shown that cynarin artichokes can help reduce blood cholesterol levels and improve liver function, and that they have a beneficial effect on the gallbladder, particularly if gallstones develop. Artichokes are also valuable because they are among the foods that seldom, if ever, trigger allergic reactions (other non-allergenic foods include pears, peaches, lettuce, apples, carrots and brown, white and wild rice).

- Artichokes are rich in folate, a group of compounds derived from folic acid, which the body needs for cell division, the formation of DNA and RNA, and protein synthesis. Folate is also vital for the healthy growth of a baby during pregnancy and the formation of the blood protein which carries oxygen from the lungs to other tissues of the body. Artichokes are thought to limit the rise in blood sugar levels after eating, and are often recommended to help diabetics.

- Globe artichokes are not related to the Jerusalem artichoke.

At the Market

- Artichokes are green in color with tightly closed leaves which are uniform in appearance. When artichokes display leaves that are beginning to open or begin to show a soft consistency, this is an indication that the freshness is gone.

Kitchen Tips

- Fresh artichokes, which remain uncut, can be refrigerated for about a week. They should be kept in tightly closed plastic bags to retain moisture. When cutting the artichoke, the use of a stainless steel knife or stainless steel scissors will prevent discoloration. Additionally, discoloration can be delayed by adding lemon juice to the cooking water.

- Although there are other methods of cooking artichokes, steaming remains a most popular method. Depending on the size of the artichoke, cooking time will vary from 30 to 60 minutes.

Artichoke Salad Recipe

INGREDIENTS:

1 12-oz. jar of artichokes in water

1/2 red onion

1 red pepper (optional)

1/4 cup black olives

5 cloves of fresh garlic

1 T parsley (fresh or diced)

1/2 cup olive oil

2 lemons (juiced)

choice of fresh herbs

DIRECTIONS:

Pour water from jar. Slice the artichokes, red onion (thin circles), red pepper, garlic, parsley, and choice of herbs. Combine in a bowl, add lemon juice and olive oil, then mix. Allow to set at least two hours. Best if marinated overnight.

BLOOD TYPE GROUPS:

 A O

Artichoke Spinach Dip Recipe

INGREDIENTS:

1 bunch of spinach

1 12-oz. jar artichoke hearts (unmarinated)

1/4 cup parmesan rice cheese

3 T rice cream cheese

2 T nutritional yeast

DIRECTIONS:

Clean spinach thoroughly. Remove stems. Blend all ingredients together in a food processor. In instances where artichokes are not indicated for your blood type, hearts of palm may be substituted.

BLOOD TYPE GROUPS:

 A O

Asparagus

Asparagus Fact Sheet

Neutral for all blood groups, asparagus is part of the onion family. Asparagus is rich in folate and also contains beta-carotene and vitamins C and E.

- Asparagus is a mild laxative and diuretic. Its high purine content means that it should be avoided by anyone with gout.

- Asparagus combines well with protein or starch.

- In *Science* magazine, Dr. Ames cited three food-based nutrients that can help us defend ourselves against cancer agents. These three, of course, include two vitamins—carotene (actually pro-vitamin A) and vitamin C—and the mineral selenium. Asparagus has all three. Asparagus benefits the heart, containing no fat, cholesterol or sodium, but containing modest amounts of cholesterol-lowering fiber.

- Containing 44 calories per cup (cooked), asparagus is ideal for healthy heart menus.

At the Market

A few tips for choosing asparagus:

- Tips should be tightly painted and purplish in color. If they are starting to open or are soft, the asparagus is past its prime.

- The stem of the asparagus should be smooth and firm.

- Asparagus that has a strong odor is too old.

Kitchen Tips

- Refrigerate asparagus as soon as you bring it home. Keep it loosely wrapped in plastic or a paper bag. To enjoy fresh asparagus year round, blanch immediately and freeze in an air-tight container. It can be frozen for 12 months.

Asparagus Soup Recipe

INGREDIENTS:

3 bunches of asparagus

Vegetable broth or bouillon (enough for two quarts of water)

2 quarts water

2 large onions

4 large cloves of garlic

DIRECTIONS:

Roast one bunch of asparagus then blend in blender with a little water. Cut and sauté vegetables in stock pot, add water, and simmer for an hour. Season to taste with liquid amino, kelp, or dulse.

BLOOD TYPE GROUPS:

Roasted Vegetables in a Sherry Vinegar Reduction Recipe

INGREDIENTS:

1 bunch of asparagus

1/2 pound brussel sprouts

2 large zucchini

3 stalks of celery

1 large red onion

1 large white onion

3 cloves of garlic

1 large bell pepper (yellow, red or orange) (optional)

8 oz. sherry vinegar

DIRECTIONS:

Preheat oven to 350°. Roast vegetables 35 minutes or until desired tenderness (except for the zucchini which goes in the last 10 minutes). If you choose to use root vegetables, roast them first for at least 10 minutes prior to adding the above-mentioned vegetables.

Reduction:

Pour 8 oz. of sherry vinegar in a saucepan and bring to a rolling boil. Reduce to simmer for 1 hour or until it reduces by half. Pour over vegetables after they have roasted. Maintain vegetables on warm until ready to serve. Makes great sandwiches.

BLOOD TYPE GROUPS:

Avacado

Avocado Fact Sheet

Neutral for A blood group but to be avoided by groups B and AB (with recommendation to avoid California varieties for blood group O), ripe avocados have positive benefits. Avocado flesh is a rich source of vitamin E and potassium and also contains useful amounts of vitamin B6, vitamin C, riboflavin, manganese and monounsaturated fats. Avocados, particularly California varieties, are high in calories. One may contain up to 400 calories. Avocados contain mainly fat, which is evidently the dominant nutrient. Avocados are classified as a fruit. Avocados contain the highest protein content of any fruit.

- They can be round, pear-shaped, or the size of an egg and weigh from 1 kg to 2 1/4 lbs.

- Depending on the variety, skin color may vary from dark green and crimson, to yellow and near-black.

Therapeutic Benefits*

- Avocados are a source of vitamin D and can help the body turn calcium into bone. There's more to avocados than guacamole. Their oil is actually patented as a treatment for some forms of dermatitis and arthritis. According to Aubrey Hampton, author of *Natural Organic Hair and Skin Care*, long-term treatment with avocado oil helps relieve eczema.

Kitchen Tips

- Unlike most other fruits, avocados start to ripen only after they have been harvested. If you buy an unripe avocado, keep it for a few days at room temperature—this will allow it to mature and the flesh will soften.

*This treatment may be applied directly to any itchy, red or irritated areas.

Avocado Pudding Recipe

INGREDIENTS:

4 avocados

1 cup frozen berries

1/2 lemon (juiced)

1/4 cup water

DIRECTIONS:

Peel avocados and place them in a blender. Add lemon juice, frozen berries and water. Blend until there is a smooth consistency. Serve.

Tastes like fruit yogurt!

BLOOD TYPE
GROUPS:

A   O

Guacamole Recipe

INGREDIENTS*:

3-4 medium avocados (soft to touch)

1 red pepper (optional)

1/4 cup nopales

1/8 cup olive oil

1 fresh lime or lemon (juiced)

3 cloves of garlic

15 sprigs of cilantro

3 green onions

1 stalk celery

1 jalapeño

DIRECTIONS:

Slice jalapeño into quarters, keeping 1/4 with seeds and removing the seeds and pith from the remaining 3/4. Cut roots off the green onion, discard and then slice remaining green onion. Chop garlic, celery and red pepper. Place all of the ingredients into a food processor and process to desired texture.

*Note that there are no seasonings present in this recipe; this is done for optimal health.

BLOOD TYPE
GROUPS:

A   O

Banana Fact Sheet

Neutral for blood groups B and O and should be avoided by AB and A blood groups, bananas are a tropical and semi-tropical fruit.

• Bananas are high in potassium. Ripe bananas are extremely digestible and aid in recovery from diarrhea and constipation. Bananas are rich in neutral sugar, which releases quickly into the blood stream.

Therapeutic Benefits

• Often athletes in need of quick energy eat bananas as a convenient snack.

• From the *Journal of Reconstructive Surgery*: A clinical trial found that scraping the inner white part of a banana peel and rubbing it into a wart 2-4 times a day for 5-7 days is helpful. Bananas are also a remedy for many gastro-intestinal problems because they soothe the digestive tract. Studies also show that bananas have an anti-ulcer effect.

At the Market

• Unripe bananas should be avoided; they contain "resistant" starch, which can not be digested in the small intestine, and starts fermenting in the small intestine, making gas as a result. As the fruit ripens, most of the starch turns into sugar, which is easier for the body to digest.

Kitchen Tips

• Often we do not consume all of the bananas we have purchased before they begin to spot or brown. Instead of throwing them away, simply freeze them. This way, there are always bananas on hand for smoothies or banana pancakes.

Banana Pancakes with Berry Syrup Recipe

INGREDIENTS:

9 frozen bananas

1/2 t vanilla (optional)

1/2 t cinnamon (optional)

1/2 cup water

Syrup:

1 cup frozen raspberries

2 dates

1-1/2 cups water

DIRECTIONS:

Soak bananas in water until they thaw. Blend in blender with water and spices. Pour batter onto lightly oiled baking sheet. Bake at 250° for 1 hour. For syrup, remove seeds from dates. Soak dates in hot water 5-8 minutes. Add dates and water to saucepan with raspberries; simmer 5 minutes. Blend in blender then pour over pancakes. Syrup can be made with other frozen fruits, carob or date ginger sauce. Cinnamon and vanilla can be used if blood type permits. To make "live" food cookies with pancake batter, dehydrate in oven on warm overnight.

BLOOD TYPE GROUPS:
B O

Banana Carob Shake Recipe

INGREDIENTS:

8 frozen bananas

2 dates

1 cup of water

3 tablespoons carob powder

DIRECTIONS:

Soak dates in warm water. Combine ingredients and blend in a blender until smooth. One cup of apple juice can be substituted for the water and dates. You can also use other fruit, such as peaches, blueberries, etc., to make different flavors.

Makes 6 - 8 Servings

BLOOD TYPE GROUPS:
B O

Basil Fact Sheet

Neutral for all blood groups, basil is a leafy herb from the mint family with a licorice-clove flavor. Basil is usually green, though there are purple varieties, such as opal basil. Lemon basil, anise basil, clove basil and cinnamon basil all have flavors similar to their names. Basil is a key ingredient in Mediterranean cooking.

Food Combining with Basil

- In food combining, herbs and spices are versatile, culinary additions that can live with proteins, starches, salads and all kinds of vegetables foods. Some herbs are classified as vegetables: the seeds of others, when ground, are classified as spices, herbs can be used freely in cooking, because of their health-giving properties. Spices however must be used sparingly in quantity. They can be a source of stomach irritation and aggravated digestive disorders.

- In cooking, sweet-tasting basil leaves are a frequent ingredient in sauces, such as pesto. Basil is also used as a vegetable garnish in soups, salads and main dishes.

Therapeutic Benefits

- Basil improves digestion, lowers fever, relaxes spasms, calms the nervous system, and is an effective remedy against bacterial infections and intestinal parasites.

- Basil is mainly a spice in this country; however, in India and Africa it is used extensively as medicine. Leaves are rubbed on the skin as an insect repellent. Drinking basil tea relieves nausea. Preparations of the herb can be applied to the skin to treat insect stings, bites, acne and other skin infections. Basil oil is used in insect repellents and in some dental preparations.

At the Market

- Available year-round, but true harvest is summer. Look for even-colored leaves.

Kitchen Tips

- Refrigerate wrapped in damp paper towels and a plastic bag for up to four days, or stems down in a glass of water with plastic over the leaves for about a week with regular water changing. Store the dried herb for 6 months in a cool, dark place. Basil is a restorative, warm, aromatic herb.

Pesto Recipe

INGREDIENTS:

4 bunches of basil Leaves

6 cloves garlic

1/4 cup olive oil

1/4 cup mozzarella or Parmesan rice cheese

1/4 cup nutritional yeast

DIRECTIONS:

Mix all ingredients together in the food processor. Serve with carrot crackers. Raw spinach can be used as a substitute for basil.

BLOOD TYPE GROUPS:
A B
AB O

Basil Dressing Recipe

INGREDIENTS:

1 cup olive oil

1/2 cup fresh basil (chopped)

3 cloves of garlic, minced

1 T grated lemon zest (grated lemon rind)

liquid amino or kelp (optional)

DIRECTIONS:

Combine the garlic, lemon zest, basil and olive oil in a mortar and grind together with a pestal until all elements are fully incorporated.

BLOOD TYPE GROUPS:
A B
AB O

Beans

Beans Fact Sheet

Legumes are remarkable in being dominated by both proteins and starches. This is, in fact, why they are difficult to digest. Raw: they are indigestible and potentially toxic because of the fascine acid they contain. Cooked: they tend to lie heavy on the stomach and they can cause some degree of flatulence. (The herb savoy may slightly reduce flatulence.)

Food Combining and Nutritional Data

- In food combining, digestion may be improved by combining beans with other types of vegetables that have the effect of restoring the acid-based balance.

- Small navy beans are a first-rate protein provider; they also contain folate, iron, phosphorus, potassium and zinc.

- Sprouted beans are an ideal constituent of any food-combining diet, since they are highly alkaline. Beans are high in fiber and low in fat—just right for lowering cholesterol. They also contain lecithin, a nutrient that helps cut cholesterol. One study showed that a cup of dried beans a day, about a bowl of bean soup, can lower total cholesterol levels by 19 percent. Phytoestrogens in beans work toward preventing breast cancer. Eat bean soup or bean salad three times a week.

Therapeutic Benefits

- Natural diabetes treatment—many studies demonstrate that eating foods that are high in soluble fiber reduces the rise in blood sugar after the meal and delays the drop in blood sugar.

Kitchen Tips

- Soak dry beans in water overnight, then discard the water and cook the soaked beans in new water.

- Tips on banishing gas: Eat more slowly; chew your food thoroughly. Eat your meal as relaxed as possible. Lactose intolerance is another major cause of flatulence; eliminate dairy products.

Adzuki Bean Soup Recipe

INGREDIENTS:

4 cups adzuki beans

1 cup of carrot pulp

1 medium onion (chopped)

1 stalk of celery (chopped)

3 cloves of garlic (chopped)

3 T chili powder

3 T BBQ seasoning

1 T baking soda

DIRECTIONS:

Soak beans overnight. Stir baking soda into soaked beans and then rinse. Cook on medium high, bringing to a rolling boil for 20 minutes, frequently removing the foam for degassing. Simmer until tender. Add garlic, onions and celery. Take 2 cups of beans from pot, place in blender with 1 cup carrot pulp, blend to smooth consistency and add back into pot. Add chili powder and/or BBQ seasoning or seasoning of choice.

BLOOD TYPE GROUPS:

A   O

Fishwich Recipe

INGREDIENTS:

3 cups steamed fish

1 cup cooked beans

1/4 cup green onion

1/4 cup onion

1/4 cup cilantro

3 cloves of garlic (shredded or minced)

1/2 t chili powder

1/2 t sage

1/2 t paprika

DIRECTIONS:

Blend all ingredients in a food processor. Shape into patties. On a greased baking dish, bake for 20 minutes on the bottom rack, then 20 minutes on the top rack. Serve on spouted pita bread.

BLOOD TYPE GROUPS:

A   O

Black Beans with Baked Spiced Goat Cheese Recipe

Most dried beans will double in size when soaked, and triple in size when cooked. Black beans are medium-sized, thick-skinned beans. Slow soak in cold water 6 hours at room temperature or quick soak (bring to a boil and cook 2 minutes; remove from heat and let soak 1 hour).

INGREDIENTS:

1 pound dried black beans (soaked)

4 cups vegetable broth

4 cups cold water

1 large onion (diced)

2 carrots

2 stalks of celery

4 cloves of garlic

1 jalapeño seeded and chopped (optional)

3 T liquid amino or kelp

1 T chili powder

1 T cumin

DIRECTIONS:

Pre-heat oven to 300°, drain and rinse. Place beans in vegetable broth, bring to a boil on top of the stove—then transfer to the oven, cover and bake for two hours. Using a skillet, add 1 cup of broth with onions, carrots, celery and garlic. Cook over medium heat until vegetables are softened. Stir the cooked vegetable mixture into the beans with chili powder, cumin, and liquid amino or kelp. Cover and bake the beans for 1 hour or until the liquid is absorbed and the beans are thoroughly cooked. Serve beans garnished with cheese and jalapeños.

BLOOD TYPE GROUPS:

A   O

Baked Spiced Goat Cheese Recipe

INGREDIENTS:

Spiced goat cheese

1/2 lb mild goat cheese

2 T red chili powder

1 cup snipped fresh chives (about 1 bunch)

DIRECTIONS:

Using a sharp knife dipped into hot water, cut 8 rounds from the goat cheese. Place chili powder and chives in small bowls. Dip 1 edge of the goat cheese rounds in the chili powder. Sprinkle the center with chives. Place the rounds—chive side up—in a covered dish. Preserve in the refrigerator until ready to bake. Bake on 300° until intended consistency is reached.

BLOOD TYPE GROUPS:

A   O

Bean Artichoke over Garlic Bread Recipe

INGREDIENTS:

4 cups cooked beans (any variety)

1 16-ounce jar of artichoke hearts (drained)

3 lemons (juiced)

3/4 cup olive oil

1 T Italian seasoning

6 garlic cloves

Bread of choice (sprouted or spelt)

DIRECTIONS:

Marinate artichoke in lemon juice, 1/2 cup of olive oil and Italian seasoning for 1 hour. Warm beans and season to taste, then add artichoke heart mixture. Add 1/4 cup of olive oil and garlic clove mixture into cream and spread on the bread, then toast in oven until brown.

Top with artichoke bean mixture.

BLOOD TYPE GROUPS:

A   O

Great Northern Hummus Recipe

INGREDIENTS:

1 16-ounce can of Great Northern Hummus

1/4 cup of fresh lemon juice

1/2 t crushed red pepper (optional)

4 T tahini

3 cloves of garlic (minced)

1 cup hot water

1/4 cup roasted red peppers (optional)

Pinch of cayenne pepper (optional)

DIRECTIONS:

Blend together ingredients in a food processor. For a spicy roasted red pepper taste, add optional ingredients. Another option is to add 1/4 cup of sliced black olives. Hummus can be served with carrot crackers. (See recipe on page 45.)

BLOOD TYPE GROUPS:

A   O

Beets

Beet Fact Sheet

Beneficial for blood groups, B and AB and neutral for A and O, beet root is rich in potassium, which helps to regulate the heartbeat and maintain normal blood pressure and nerve function. Beets are a good source of folate and contain some vitamin C. Fresh, raw beetroot (beet) juice is such a concentrated vitamin and mineral resource that it is considered a perfect tonic for convalescents. Medical researchers have reason to think beets contain valuable anti-carcinogens. The sugar in beets acts as an appetite suppressant; the fiber makes people feel full. Beets are an extrinsic sugar; therefore, the official view is that they should not exceed more than 10 percent of total daily intake, because of sugar content

- Beet greens—the edible leafy tips—contain beta-carotene, calcium and iron. However, if boiled, they lose much of their vitamin C content, which leeches away in the water.

- Beet greens can be shredded and added to soups. They will impart a red color to the broth.

Therapeutic Benefits

- Beet juice therapy for psoriasis: Those who suffer with psoriasis have congestion in the bowels and liver. A high-fiber diet will absorb toxins in the gut and the beet juice will help detoxify. Drink one glass of this mixture daily—1 beet to 4 carrots and 1/4 of a lemon.

Ginger Beet Salad Recipe

INGREDIENTS:

2 cups grated beets

2 t grated ginger root

1 T maple syrup

1 T liquid amino or

1 T lemon juice

Clover sprouts

DIRECTIONS:

In a small bowl combine beets, ginger, maple syrup, liquid amino, sprouts and lemon juice. Toss and let flavors blend.

BLOOD TYPE
GROUPS:

BBQ Sauce Recipe

INGREDIENTS:

4 carrots

2 beets

3 cloves of garlic

1 stalk of celery

3 onions

1 cup carrot juice

1/2 cup beet juice

3 T BBQ seasoning

1 t liquid amino

DIRECTIONS:

Preheat oven to 350°. Roast root vegetables for 10 minutes, then add above ground vegetables and continue roasting for another 30 minutes or until desired tenderness. Blend roasted vegetables in a food processor with BBQ seasoning and liquid amino. Pour contents into a blender and blend with beet juice. Add more BBQ seasoning to taste. Liquid Smoke® flavor can also be added if desired.

BLOOD TYPE
GROUPS:

Carrots

Carrot Fact Sheet

Beneficial for blood groups A and B and neutral for O and AB, carrots are a good source of beta-carotene, which the body turns into vitamin A. Carrots are better eaten juiced or cooked than raw. Cooking breaks down the cell walls, making absorbing the vitamin A easier and therefore does not effect beta-carotene levels.

Nutritional Data

- 1 cup of raw, shredded carrots provides 31,000 international units of vitamin A. Carrots are a good source of potassium (cooked or raw), are virtually fat-free and are high in soluble fiber. One carrot—7 1/2 inches long and 1 1/18 inch in diameter—yields the following nutrients: 25 grams of calcium, 26 grams of phosphorus, 0.5 grams of iron, 34 grams of sodium, 246 grams of potassium, 7,930 IU vitamin A, trace amounts of vitamin B complex and 6 grams of vitamin C.

Therapeutic Benefits

- Carrots can help your vision; they assist you in seeing better in poor light. Vitamin A-rich carrots help your eyes adjust from light to darkness. Vitamin A also assists the liver in removing the toxins from the body. Carrot juice is sufficiently rich in potassium to help neutralize excess acid. Beta-carotene-rich foods reduce the risk of cancer of the lungs, stomach, mouth and prostate.

At the Market

- For best taste, choose carrots that are small-to-medium in size and tapered at the tips. Carrots should have a bright orange color and firm texture. Limpness, sprouts on the carrot or signs of decay on the tips are signs that the carrot has started to break down. Greens at the top of the carrot are signs of freshness.

Kitchen Tips

- When storing carrots, remove tops that are present. Store the carrots in plastic in the refrigerator, keep carrots away from apples when storing to prevent bitterness. A good batch of carrots will keep 2-3 weeks. One pound of carrots yields 4 cups shredded. For fast cooking, cut into coin-shaped pieces and steam for about 10 minutes until tender. For more taste, cut carrots on a diagonal.

Carrot Pulp Crackers Recipe

INGREDIENTS:

2 cups carrot pulp

1/2 t spike

1/2 t garlic

1/2 t onion

1/2 t parsley

DIRECTIONS:

Form patties and spread on the dehydrator shelves or in an oven on a cookie sheet (lowest temperature for oven or warm setting).

Dehydrate for 18-24 hours. and cook in oven for 2-3 hours. They are done when brittle like a chip or cracker and can be used to dip.

A variety of herbs can be included in the carrot pulp recipe—for instance, dill, basil, rosemary, ginger, curry and any other seasoning can be used to produce the desired flavor.

BLOOD TYPE
GROUPS:

Carrot Pulp Burgers Recipe

INGREDIENTS:

2 cups any bean (cooked and drained)

1 cup carrot pulp

1/4 cup onions (diced)

1/4 cup celery (diced)

1 t granulated garlic

1 t granulated onion

1 t spike

liquid amino (optional)

DIRECTIONS:

Mix all ingredients well, shape into 4, 6-oz. patties. Broil or bake (350°) in a little oil. Flip when half-done to cook opposite sides. Serve with sautéed onions and garlic.

Carrot pulp can also be used in adzuki beans in order to achieve the desired flavor. Add 2–4 cups, depending on the amount of beans you are preparing.

BLOOD TYPE
GROUPS:

Carrot Ginger Apple Juice Recipe

INGREDIENTS:

6 lbs. carrots

9 apples

1/2 lb. ginger

DIRECTIONS:

Peel carrots with a vegetable peeler. Cut apples into pieces to fit in juicer, slice ginger. Juice ginger, carrots, apples, and pour together into a gallon container. Serve. For optimum enzyme consumption, serve within 20 minutes of preparation; otherwise store in freezer. Enzymes begin to dissipate in fresh juice after 20 minutes and are slightly negligible after 12 hours. To make apple sauce, peel and core the apples; save the pulp. For carrot pulp clean juicer and save pulp. If you're not going to save the pulp, juice the ginger first.

Makes 3 1/2 quarts to a gallon.

BLOOD TYPE GROUPS:

A B
AB O

Carrot Apple Beet Juice Recipe

When juicing any fruit or vegetable, be sure to cut it into pieces small enough for your juicer to handle. For example, an apple may be cored and cut into quarters. You can leave the peels on, the juicer will separate them out during juicing. To strain out any indigestible pulp or fiber that is not separated from the juice by the juicer, pour the fresh juice through a wire mesh stainless steel strainer.

INGREDIENTS:

8-10 medium carrots (washed and trimmed and unpeeled) Yield: about 3 cups of fresh juice

2 large apples (washed, cored and unpeeled) Yield: about 2 cups of fresh juice

1 large beet (washed and trimmed and unpeeled) Yield: about 1/2 cup of fresh juice

DIRECTIONS:

Cut apples and beets into pieces. Juice with the carrots in a high speed juicer. Strain out pulp using wire mesh strainer and serve.

BLOOD TYPE GROUPS:

A B
AB O

Celery

Celery Fact Sheet

Therapeutic Benefits

Beneficial for A and AB and neutral to B and O blood groups, celery is extremely low in calories and is a good source of potassium. Studies have shown that the anti-inflammatory agents in celery can reduce the symptoms of gout, while the sedative compound in it can help to lower blood pressure.

- Celery juice has a mild diuretic effect, similar to many drugs that are prescribed for high blood pressure. An 8-ounce blend of one-part celery juice, one-part carrot juice and one-part water, taken daily is highly nutritious and can be helpful for people with high blood pressure.

- Celery juice is rich in substances that have a soothing effect on the vascular system and this may benefit those prone to migraines. Celery juice has a very soothing effect on the nervous system and is a wonderful tonic for the person with a "Type A" personality.

Nutritional Data

- Three stalks of fresh celery a day provide enough natural sodium for the digestive system to operate properly.

- Celery contains calcium blockers and other plant chemicals (phytochemicals)—such as magnesium and potassium that help treat and prevent arrhythmias, flus and other compounds that lower cholesterol.

Vegetable Stock Recipe

INGREDIENTS:

3 onions

3 stalks of celery

5 cloves of garlic

2 T paprika

2 T granulated garlic

2 T onion powder

2 T of nutritional yeast

1/2 t of kelp powder

8 cups boiling water

Vegetables of choice such as zucchini, carrots, broccoli, etc.

DIRECTIONS:

Chop vegetables and sauté in stock pot; slowly add three cups of boiling water when vegetables begin to stick. Add seasoning, mix thoroughly, and add 3 more cups of boiling water. Bring to a boil. Add nutritional yeast, then add two more cups of boiling water; turn down to simmer for 30 minutes. Strain vegetables from broth and blend in blender. Add blended vegetables to stock and simmer for 15 minutes.

BLOOD TYPE GROUPS:
A B
AB O

Roasted Vegetable Soup Recipe

INGREDIENTS:

3 stalks of celery

1 large red onion

1 large white onion

3 cloves garlic

1 large yellow, red or orange bell pepper (optional)

2 carrots (sliced)

1 turnip (sliced)

Sliced vegetables of choice: asparagus, brussels sprouts, zucchini etc.

6 cups vegetable stock

DIRECTIONS:

Preheat oven to 350°. Roast root vegetables 10 minutes then add above ground vegetables, continue roasting for 20 minutes or until desired tenderness (except for zucchini, which goes in last 10 minutes). Heat vegetable stock; add roasted vegetables. Another option is to blend roasted vegetables before adding to stock.

BLOOD TYPE GROUPS:
A B
AB O

Chocolate Fact Sheet

Neutral to all blood groups, chocolate really can boost levels of body chemicals that make you feel good, according to Debra Waterknuse, author of *Why Women Crave Chocolate*. These chemicals include the neurotransmitter, serotonin and endorphins, which relieve pain and boost moods. All brain chemicals are positioned at optimal levels for positive moods and renewed energy.

About Cocoa

• Cocoa powder is made from the part of the cocoa bean that harbors flavonoids.

• Flavonoids are potent plant antioxidants and can exert a positive influence on health by neutralizing damaging free radicals, substances thought to advance aging and promote disease.

• Roasting cocoa beans and fermenting them (two processes that help develop flavor), can destroy some of the flavonoid compounds. Fifty to 75 percent of flavonoids are lost during the traditional processing of most chocolates. The heat and alkaline products used to treat the cocoa destroys flavonoids. When heat and alkalization are reduced during processing, approximately 90 to 95 percent of flavonoids are preserved.

• A major emollient used in skin lotions and cosmetics, cocoa butter is the natural leading anti-wrinkle recommendation of Natural Pharmacist Albert Leung, Ph.D. It melts at body temperature and moisturizes dry skin, especially around the eyes (crow's feet), the corners of the mouth and on the neck.

Therapeutic Benefits

• Researchers identifying flavonoids in chocolates found sub-class flavonoids, a compound with health benefits. A German study found that eating dark chocolate high in flavonoids may reduce blood pressure. Small daily doses of flavonoid-rich chocolate can improve blood flow and blood vessel health. Dark chocolate harbors the highest amounts of these compounds.

At the Market

• Look for the highest amount of flavonoids, choose products with high cocoa content, 70 percent or greater.

Chocolate Cups & Dipped Apples Recipe

INGREDIENTS:

1 lb. chocolate or carob (optional)

6-8 small drinking cups

4 apples (sliced)

DIRECTIONS:

Melt chocolate in a double broiler. A double broiler consists of a saucepan with boiling water and a bowl covering the saucepan. Melt the chocolate in a bowl. Once the chocolate is melted, pour into small Dixie water cups, covering the inside surface with chocolate. Place in refrigerator to harden. Dip apples or other fruit in remaining chocolate and refrigerate to harden. It takes about an hour. Peel the cups away from the chocolate after they have hardened. Place fruit inside and serve. If you use apples or pears, soak briefly in lemon water so that they don't turn brown. Also, the cups can be filled with a variety of things, such as maple almonds, lemon pudding, avocado pudding, berries, or any other ideas you may have. Be creative.

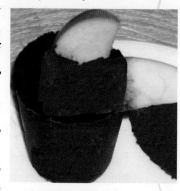

BLOOD TYPE
GROUPS:
A B
AB O

Bittersweet Chocolate Sorbet Recipe

INGREDIENTS:

2 cups water

1 cup maple syrup

1/2 cup unsweetened cocoa

3 oz. of bittersweet chocolate (finely chopped)

2 t of vanilla extract

DIRECTIONS:

Bring water to a boil in medium saucepan. Stir in maple syrup and cocoa; reduce heat and simmer for five minutes, stirring frequently. Remove from heat; add chocolate and vanilla, stirring until chocolate melts. Cover and chill completely.

Pour mixture into ice cream freezer and freeze according to manufacturer's instructions. Spoon sorbet into a freezer-safe container, cover and freeze for one hour or until firm. Makes 6 servings.

BLOOD TYPE
GROUPS:
A B
AB O

Dates

Date Fact Sheet

Neutral to blood groups A, B, AB and O, the date is a fruit from a tall palm tree known as the date palm. In ancient times, the date tree was symbolic of moral uprightness and heaven-sent prosperity. Dates are still the staff of life for people who dwell in the arid regions of North Africa and the Middle East.

- The Date Palm bears its first fruit in the fourth year and continues to do so, with little or no care, and under far from ideal growing conditions, for the next 75 years.

Nutritional Data

- Ten dates yield the following nutrients: 47 mg calcium, 50 mg phosphorus, 2.4 mg of iron, 1 mg sodium, 518 mg potassium, 40 I.U., vitamins A, 1.8 mg niacin and very little vitamin C.

Therapeutic Benefits

- Celiac Disease, also called Sprue, is classified as a malabsorption syndrome. Celiac Disease is a chronic intestinal disorder in which intolerance to gluten (a protein found in grains) interferes with the proper absorption of many nutrients. Dates contain unique protein carbohydrate complexes and mineral salts which halt an abnormal response started by gluten in the small intestine, leading to overproduction of white blood cells. The spice cardamom works in the same way and can be used along with dates as a flavoring and medicinal agent.

At the Market

- Choose plump, soft dates with a smooth, shiny skin. Avoid very shriveled dates or those with mold or sugar crystals on the skin.

Kitchen Tips

- Store fresh dates, wrapped in a plastic bag, in the refrigerator up to 2 weeks. Dried dates can be stored, airtight, at room temperature in a cool, dry place for up to 6 months or up to a year in the refrigerator.

Ginger Date Sauce Recipe

INGREDIENTS:

6 dates

1 1/2 cups water

1/4 cup fresh ginger juice

2 lemons (juiced)

DIRECTIONS:

Cover dates with water. Soak dates overnight. Remove seeds from dates. Blend dates, date water, ginger juice and lemon juice in blender. Heat mixture on stove.

BLOOD TYPE GROUPS:

A   B
AB   O

Date Rolls Recipe

INGREDIENTS:

1 cup almonds (grated)

2 cups dates (grated)

DIRECTIONS:

In a food processor, blend dates and 1/2 cup of ground almonds. Form this mixture into date-shaped balls and then roll them onto ground almonds.

BLOOD TYPE GROUPS:

A   B
AB   O

Eggplant

Eggplant Fact Sheet

Eggplant is neutral for blood groups O, B and AB and should be avoided by the A blood group. A member of the nightshade family, eggplant is related to the potato and tomato. Though commonly thought of as a vegetable, eggplant is actually a fruit, specifically a berry. There are many varieties of this delicious food, ranging in color from rich purple to white, in length from 2-12 inches, and in shape from oblong to round. In the United States, the most common eggplant is the large, cylindrical-or pear-shaped variety with a smooth, glossy, dark purple skin.

Nutritional Data

- Eggplants are very low in saturated fat, cholesterol and sodium. They are a good source of vitamin C, vitamin K, thiamin, niacin, vitamin B6, pantothenic acid, magnesium, phosphorus and copper, and a very good source of dietary fiber, folate, potassium and manganese.

At the Market

- Look for smooth, shiny skin with a firm but slightly springy texture. Avoid soft or brown spots.

Kitchen Tips

- Eggplants become bitter with age and are very perishable. They should be stored in a cool, dry place and used within a day or two of purchase. If longer storage is necessary, place the eggplant in the refrigerator vegetable drawer. Eggplant can be prepared in a variety of ways, including baking and broiling. It does, however, have a spongelike capacity to soak up oil so it should be well-coated with a spelt batter or a sprouted bread crumb mixture to inhibit fat absorption.

Eggplant Pizza Recipe

INGREDIENTS:

3 large eggplants

1 bunch of fresh basil

1 pack of dry sun-dried tomatoes (soak in olive oil overnight)

2 cups of marinara sauce or stewed tomatoes with garlic, Italian seasoning and minced onion

1 yellow or red pepper (sliced) (optional)

1/4 cup of either nutritional yeast (tastes like cheese) goat cheese, or rice mozzarella.

liquid amino to taste

DIRECTIONS:

Pre-heat oven to 400°. Rinse and dry eggplant, cut into round even slices about 1/2 inch thick. Place on a non-stick sheet. Brush exposed cut surfaces with olive oil and liquid amino. Bake for 6 minutes. Remove eggplant and place sauce and soaked sun-dried tomatoes on top, add fresh basil and sliced peppers. Sprinkle pizza with pizza or Italian seasoning and nutritional yeast and goat cheese. Pizza can be prepared up to this point a few hours in advance. Return to oven for 15 minutes.

BLOOD TYPE GROUPS:

B

AB   O

Cured Eggplant Recipe

INGREDIENTS:

2 medium eggplants

1-2 cups vinegar of your choice

1 medium red bell pepper (optional)

1/2 cup fresh basil (chopped)

1 T minced garlic

olive oil (enough to cover the amount of eggplant)

2 jars (one that can fit into the other with the lid on)

DIRECTIONS:

Slice eggplant horizontally into very thin slices. Place slices in the larger, wide mouth jar with a tight sealing lid. Add enough vinegar to cover all the slices.

Get a smaller jar with a lid that will fit into the mouth of the wide-mouth jar, fill it with water and seal with a lid. Put the smaller jar on top of the eggplant slices (in the larger jar) to weigh them down. Allow the weighted-down eggplant to marinate in a cool dry place for 2-4 days. Squeeze all moisture from the eggplant and clean the wide-mouth jar. Return the slices to the clean wide-mouth jar. Add red bell pepper, basil and garlic. Fill the jar with enough olive oil to cover the contents. Seal the jar and store in a cool place. The eggplant will be ready in 2-3 days; however for a deep-cured taste, wait 6 weeks. Cured eggplant keeps indefinitely, however once the jar is opened, it must be refrigerated. Makes about 3 cups.

BLOOD TYPE GROUPS:

B

AB   O

Fig

Fig Fact Sheet

Beneficial for A, AB and O—neutral for B blood groups—fresh figs are found in two varieties, black and green. Due to the easy bruising of figs, they do not travel well, and are more difficult to find. Dried figs are more commonly found in supermarkets. The drying process serves to concentrate the useful nutrients that figs naturally contain. They are rich in potassium and also contain useful amounts of calcium and iron. Their high fiber content is also valuable, which comes in two forms: pectin which is a soluble variety that can assist in lowering levels of cholesterol in the blood; insoluble, which helps promote the movement of food through the colon and assists in the prevention of constipation. Eating just a handful of dried figs will usually have a laxative effect, and the syrup of figs is a traditional remedy to treat constipation.

Nutritional Data

- This fruit's drawback is that when it is dried it is rich in sugar, and if eaten too often, may contribute to tooth decay: 37 calories per medium fig raw, 143 calories per 3 dried figs.

Therapeutic Benefits

- In the Bible, when King Solomon developed boils, his physicians applied figs. This is one of the few descriptions of the medicinal usage of figs in the Bible. Figs contain protein-dissolving enzymes that help dissolve unwanted skin growths, including corns.

- To remove corns or other growths, open fresh figs and apply the pulp to the growth overnight. The following morning, remove and soak feet in hot water. After 1 hour, try to remove the corn. It should come off easily; in stubborn cases, 4-5 overnight treatments may be required.

- The same protealytic enzyme known as ficin in figs has been used in many cases for treatment of warts. Apply juice once a day for 5-7 days.

- A recent study on fiber, conducted by June Kelsay, Ph.D., of the U.S. Department of Agriculture, tested 3 diets containing progressively higher amounts of fiber from foods such as figs. The calorie count of each diet was the same—subjects complained of being asked to eat too much food when the diet contained more figs. Eat more figs and want less food.

Kitchen Tips

- For fresh figs, store in the refrigerator loosely covered—they will not keep long but will last a couple days. Keep dried figs, Calimigrina or Black Mension, in the freezer, refrigerator or cool, dark pantry. The approximate digestion time is 1 1/2-2 hours.

Almond Figs Recipe

INGREDIENTS:

12 ounces of dried black figs

1/4 cup apricot nectar

1 T lemon juice

2 drops almond extract

2 T toasted, slivered almonds

DIRECTIONS:

If figs have stems, remove with knife. Place figs in non-metal bowl and add nectar and juice. Cover and marinate in refrigerator overnight.

In a small saucepan, simmer figs and marinade with almond extract over medium heat until figs are heated and appear plump (about 4 minutes). Sprinkle with almonds.

Serve warm or hot, for breakfast or dessert.

BLOOD TYPE GROUPS:

Fig Jelly Recipe

INGREDIENTS:

1 lb fresh or dried figs

Water

4 T date sugar

OR

6 fresh dates

DIRECTIONS:

Soak figs in water overnight. Water should cover figs. Stew for 30 minutes. If you choose to use fresh dates, soak them for 30 minutes. Combine dates or date sugar with figs in food processor; blend until smooth consistency. Serve over fresh or stewed fruit of your choice.

BLOOD TYPE GROUPS:

Nana Newtons Recipe

INGREDIENTS:

2 bananas (or fruit of choice)

1/4 cup water (enough water to moisten for blending)

DIRECTIONS:

Blend fruit and water. Pour 1/4 inch thick into a silicon muffin pan and dehydrate in oven at 170°. This usually takes all night.

Fill with fig jelly (refer to Fig Jelly Recipe on page 61.)

For wafers, spread banana of fruit batter across plastic wrap.

BLOOD TYPE
GROUPS:

Fig and Date Cake Recipe

This is a 4-part recipe—assembly required!

INGREDIENTS:

Part 1

1 cup dates

1 cup figs

1/2 cup date sugar

1 1/2 T raw carob powder

1/2 T vanilla extract

[Soak dates and figs in filtered water, covering them. Use this water in recipe.]

Part 2

2 cups fresh or frozen peaches

1 1/2 cup almonds

1/2 cup maple syrup

1 T vanilla extract (optional)

Combine these ingredients in a blender and blend well

Part 3

2 cups warm frozen or fresh peaches

Part 4

3 cups maple syrup

2/3 cup olive oil

1 cup raw carob powder

2 T of vanilla extract (optional)

DIRECTIONS:

Combine in blender — blend well.

Soak dates and dried figs in water for two hours, then drain. Blend dates, figs, maple syrup, vanilla extract and raw carob powder in a food processor.

Divide the date mixture in half and form each of the halves into a 4-inch diameter, circular mini cake. Place on a desert plate. Set aside.

Pour Part 2 of this recipe over the fig and date cakes. Put the peaches in Part 3 of this recipe over the cake and sauce. Put the sauce in Part 4 of this recipe over everything and enjoy!

BLOOD TYPE
GROUPS:

Ginger

Ginger Fact Sheet

Beneficial for A, B and O blood groups, also neutral for AB, Ginger is one of more than 1,400 species, belonging to the Zingiberaceae family. Ginger is a slender perennial. The most familiar part of the ginger plant is the irregularly shaped and sized underground section which is erroneously called a root. It is botanically correct to call it rhizome. Almost as distinctive as ginger's taste is its fragrance: a sweet, warm, citrus aroma, highly regarded and widely used in perfumes.

Nutritional Data

- Vitamins/Minerals (milligrams/100 grams).................................. B1-.06
- Calcium -20.00... B2-03
- Phosphorus-60.00.. B3-.60
- Iron-2.60 .... C-6.00

Nutritional value for dry ginger depends on the reduction of moisture.

Therapeutic Benefits

- Some of ginger's most remarkable effects occur in the digestive system. It can be used to treat anorexia, flatulence (gas), gastric and intestinal spasms, acute colds and painful menstruation. It works well for abdominal cramps, nausea (traveling and morning sickness), blood circulation and lung congestion, promotes perspiration and urination and is a lymph gland purifier—along with many more. Ginger aids the male reproductive system; it stimulates the hormonal levels of the body, significantly changing the sperm motility in the body. Ginger poses an anthelmintic effect, including activities against some of the world's most widespread and dangerous parasites.

Food Combining

- Ginger dry or fresh combines with all food categories

- The key part of the plant is the rhizome (root), which can be used fresh in syrups, crystallized as candies or dried and ground into powder for cooking. Fresh ginger can be used to flavor rice dishes, cookies, cakes, biscuits and sauces.

At the Market

- Ginger should be evenly colored, non-spongy to touch, and devoid of new sprouts (although useable, sprouts indicate ginger is past its prime or old).

Kitchen Tips

- Once ginger is cleaned, it is not necessary to peel unless specified by recipe.

Ginger Beer Recipe

INGREDIENTS:

1 1/2 lb. ginger

22 lemons or limes

2 cups maple syrup

DIRECTIONS:

Juice the ginger, squeeze lemons or limes, mix in a gallon container, and fill the difference with water and blend. Serve frosted or steaming. Makes one gallon.

BLOOD TYPE
GROUPS:

Ginger Carrot Soup Recipe

INGREDIENTS:

4 lbs carrots

1/4 lb ginger

1 medium-sized onion

3 cloves of garlic

2 stalks of celery

3 T paprika

2 T granulated garlic

2 T onion powder

1 T curry powder

6-8 cups of boiling water (based on desired thickness)

DIRECTIONS:

Peel ginger. Slice carrots, ginger, garlic, and celery. Dice onion. Heat stock pot and sauté sliced and diced vegetables. Add seasoning, pouring in 2 cups of water at a time. Fold in all ingredients. Simmer approximately 30 minutes or until carrots have softened. Blend ingredients in blender until smooth. Return to pot and simmer 15 minutes. Serves 8.

BLOOD TYPE
GROUPS:

Gingersnaps Recipe

INGREDIENTS:

1/4 cup ginger

2 cups spelt flour

1 1/4 cups maple crystals

3/4 cup water

1/3 cup olive oil

2 t vanilla extract

1 t cinnamon (optional)

1 t molasses

1 t baking soda

1/2 t salt

1/4 t nutmeg (optional)

DIRECTIONS:

Mix all the wet ingredients together in mixing bowl. In a separate bowl, combine all dry ingredients. Add dry ingredients to wet ingredients, slowly, while stirring. Mix until cookie dough forms. Scoop small cookie dough rounds on a lightly greased cookie sheet. Bake at 350° for 15 minutes or until crispy. Makes approximately 45 small cookies.

BLOOD TYPE GROUPS:

Ginger Zucchini with Carrot Shreds Recipe

INGREDIENTS:

1 lb. small zucchinis

3/4 cup shredded carrots

1/4 cup shredded red bell peppers (optional)

3 T water

1 1/2 T of finely shredded fresh ginger

1 t spike

1 t olive oil

DIRECTIONS:

Cut the zucchini in half lengthwise, then place the cut side down on the cutting board and cut lengthwise into thin slices. Cut the slice into 2-inch lengths.

Heat water to simmer in skillet or wok, add zucchini and cook, stirring every 30 seconds. Add the carrot shreds, the pepper shreds and ginger and stir for another 15 seconds or so. Add spike and continue to stir until vegetables are slightly softened, but crunchy. Turn off heat, sprinkle with olive oil and serve.

BLOOD TYPE GROUPS:

Grapes

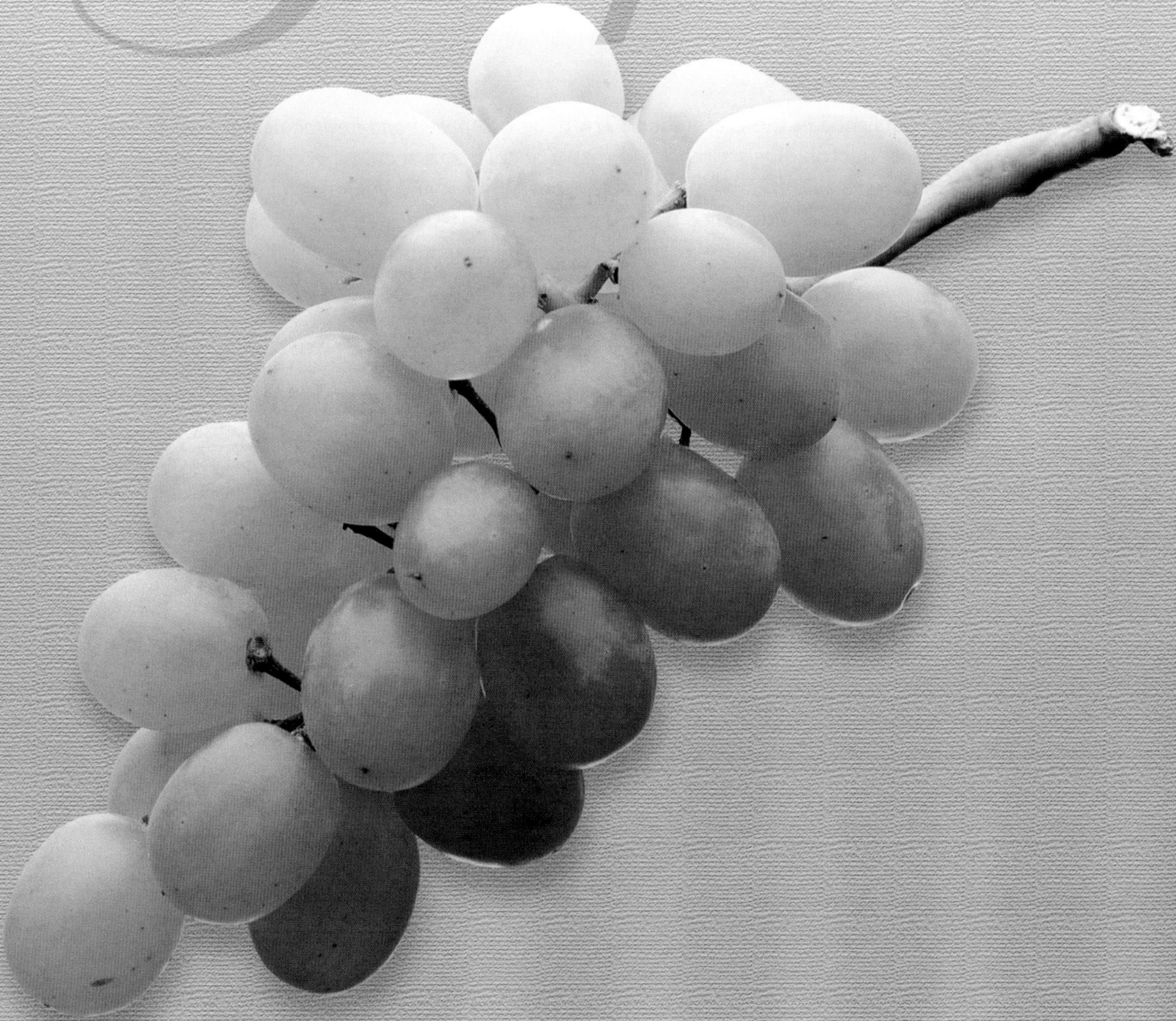

Grapes Fact Sheet

Beneficial for blood groups B and AB, and neutral for groups A and O, grapes grow on woody, climbing vines. Grape leaves are palmately lobed, usually medium-green to blue-green, lush and dramatic—turning yellow in the fall.

Nutritional Data

- One cup of grape juice contains:

  28 mg calcium, 30 mg phosphorus, 0.8 mg iron, 5 mg sodium, 293 mg potassium and small amounts of vitamins A, B-complex, C and P.

Therapeutic Benefits

- In a study published in the December 1976 issue of *Applied and Environmental Microbiology*, two Canadian microbiologists reported that Concord and seedless grape juices and red and white wines were able to inhibit cholera, herpes simplex and influenza viruses, among others. Dark grapes work best. Juice them with their seeds and then strain the liquid. One cup of fresh, dark grape juice each day can control herpes simplex virus conditions.

At the Market

- When shopping for table grapes, it is imperative to remember the fruit does not ripen any further, nor does the taste improve, once it has been severed from the vine. What you see—or better, what you taste at the time of purchase—is what you get. The quicker you use them, the better—because as they age they lose crispness and flavor. Look for firm, plump, colorful, dry berries that are firmly attached to the pliable green stems.

Stewed Grapes Recipe

INGREDIENTS:

1 lb grapes

1 t date sugar

DIRECTIONS:

In a stainless steel pot, on low heat, place grapes and smash them with the back of serving spoon. After you have some juice, bring it to a simmer and add date sugar.

Transitional Recipes for Food Combining & Blood Typing

Grape Pie Recipe

Crust Ingredients:
1-2 cups almonds (soak 8-12 hours)
3-4 T maple syrup

This crust is good for soft fillings or frozen pies. One cup will yield a very thin crust; two cups will be approximately the thickness of a traditional crust. Use two cups of almonds if you are using a nine inch (22.5 cm) pie pan.

DIRECTIONS:

Drain almonds after soaking; dry them 30-60 minutes in the oven on warm. Chop in the food processor until uniformly very fine. Gradually add maple syrup, using just enough for the almond meal to hold together. Sprinkle the mixture into an 8-9-inch pie pan and then gently press it into the bottom and up the sides.

Filling Ingredients:
2 lbs. (or 5 cups) red or green seedless grapes
1/2 cup maple crystals
1/2 cup apple juice
1/2 cup apple pectin (see (Apple Facts'')

1 T lemon juice
3 T water
1/4 t nutmeg

DIRECTIONS:

Stem and rinse grapes well in apple cider vinegar, rinse with water and drain. Place them in a 2-quart stainless steel pot with apple juice. Bring to a boil, cover and cook over medium heat about 5 minutes. Press the grapes with the back of a wooden spoon to burst about half of them, releasing juice.

Pour the grapes into a strainer and then drain over a measuring cup. Measure the juice; approximately 1 1/4 cups. Return the strained pulp and skins to the saucepan along with 1 cup of juice. In a small bowl, mix apple pectin, lemon juice and water. Add this mixture to the grapes in a saucepan. Add nutmeg and maple crystals. Stir and bring to a boil over medium heat, uncovered, until it is thick and clear; about 3 minutes total time. Pour into a pie pan, allow to cool and serve.

Transitional Recipes for Food Combining & Blood Typing

Grapefruit *and* Orange

Grapefruit & Orange Fact Sheet

Grapefruits are beneficial for blood groups A and AB, and neutral for blood groups B and O. Oranges are neutral for blood group B only.

Nutritional Data

- Citrus fruits, grapefruits and oranges are particularly high in vitamin C. Oranges also contain thiamin and folate. Citrus fruits are good sources of calcium and beta carotene.

- The pith and membranes are rich in: pectin which may help to lower blood cholesterol levels; and bioflavonoids, which have powerful anti-oxidant properties. For this reason, it is better to eat the fruit rather than drink the juice. It is also better not to discard the pulp when juicing.

Therapeutic Benefits

- Grapefruit is a great food for fighting a cold, Dr. Paul Yanich, a research scientist in Milford, Pennsylvania, explains one reason: it is high in vitamin C and grapefruit helps to detoxify the liver. The liver is your frontline to the immune system, and when immunity is impaired, you need something that is alkaline and not acidic to detoxify it. All citrus fruits become alkaline when metabolized in the body, he explains; however, oranges and other fruits are too sweet to promote proper liver drainage. There is much better detoxification from grapefruits. Dr. Yanich recommends eating one or more grapefruit and their white bitter pulp each day to prevent colds and build immunity.

Berry Grapefruit Breakfast Delight Recipe

INGREDIENTS:

1 cup date sugar

2 cups cranberries

3 grapefruits (peeled and sectioned)

1 cup water

DIRECTIONS:

In a saucepan, combine date sugar and water; boil; stir to dissolve sugar. Boil for 5 minutes. Add cranberries; cook until skins pop (about 5 more minutes). Remove from heat and chill. Pour cranberry mixture over grapefruit sections in individual servings bowls. Makes 6 servings.

BLOOD TYPE GROUPS:
A B
AB O

Citrus Salad Recipe

INGREDIENTS:

1 grapefruit

1/2 pineapple

1 orange (optional)

1 tablespoon liquid or granulated lecithin

DIRECTIONS:

Peel and skin the grapefruit, orange and pineapple. Add 2 tablespoons of date sugar and mix well. Place this mixture in a baking dish and top with 1 tablespoon of lecithin (this tastes very similar to butter). Then place it in the oven and broil for 3 minutes. Enjoy!

BLOOD TYPE GROUPS:
A B
AB O

Horseradish

Horseradish Fact Sheet

Beneficial for blood groups A and O, and neutral to groups B and AB, horseradish is an unattractive and weedy plant that is a member of the mustard family. With a very strong sharp and pungent flavor (usually diluted with vinegar), it grows 2-3 feet tall and is adorned with small, white flowers. Large amounts of commercial crops are grown in the Mississippi Valley, particularly in Missouri; it is also grown on the Eastern seaboard.

Nutritional Data

- 1 teaspoon of raw, freshly ground horseradish root is very high in sulfur and potassium, with medium amounts of sodium, calcium and phosphorus, and trace amounts of iron, magnesium, copper and vitamins A, B-complex, C and E.

Therapeutic Benefits

- It is a very effective way of breaking up congestion in head and chest; this is also used to treat sinus conditions, bronchitis, chronic obstructive sinusitis, pulmonary disease, common cold/sore throat, indigestion, heartburn and allergies. For mucous congestion, soak both feet in hot water while internally taking 3-5 teaspoons of horseradish juice, flavored with maple syrup, if necessary. The very potent sulfur vapors will strip phlegm from mucosal tissue walls and promote a rapid discharge of mucous from the body —from the nose, mouth, urinary tract and colon. For sinus headaches, use 1 teaspoon straight horseradish, pulverized and mixed with 1/4 freshly-squeezed lemon. Caution: while consuming, stand near a sink because the result is rapid. If the headache persists, repeat up to 3 times throughout the day until sinuses are cleared. For allergy symptoms, use fresh or prepared horseradish. Take a daily dose of 1 tablespoon until the symptoms subside. Take once or twice a month to prevent future attacks. Caution: This is extremely hot and spicy!

Food Combining with Horseradish

- Horseradish combines with proteins or carbohydrates.

Kitchen Tips

- Horseradish is very dirty when purchased fresh—be sure to scrub thoroughly and peel before processing. It is so pungent that it causes eyes to water (like onions). Handle with caution.

- For obtaining horseradish juice or sauce, use a Vitamix®, food blender or food processor. First wash and scrub all the dirt from the root. Peel, then grate or chop into small pieces, then blend with lemon or lime juice. Store in the refrigerator in a closed container. This can be taken every 4 hours after it has been moistened with lemon or lime juice. Large discharges of tears from the eyes and mucous from the sinus cavity will take place.

Horseradish Sauce Recipe

INGREDIENTS:

Horseradish root (washed and peeled; grated or chopped)

1 medium-sized fresh turnip (washed and peeled; chopped)

1 bottle brown rice vinegar

DIRECTIONS:

Combine all ingredients into the food processor and blend until sauce consistency. (Note: When you buy the sauce from the store, salt and some form of sweetener has been added; this is not necessary.)

BLOOD TYPE
GROUPS:

Horseradish Salad Dressing Recipe

INGREDIENTS:

3 T of horseradish sauce

8 ounces olive oil

Juice of 1 lemon

3 cloves of garlic

3 T of Veganaise® or eggless mayonnaise

DIRECTIONS:

Combine all ingredients into a blender and blend until smooth, adjust olive oil amounts to reach your own preferred consistency. Pour maple syrup in a little at a time until mixture is smooth.

BLOOD TYPE
GROUPS:

Herb Mustard Recipe

INGREDIENTS:

2 T chopped parsley

2 T chopped chervil

2 T chopped chives

2 T chopped celery leaves

2 T chopped tarragon

2 T chopped thyme

7 cloves of garlic

1 T horseradish (optional for hot mustard)

sherry vinegar to cover herbs

4 ounces mustard powder

4 ounces olive oil

DIRECTIONS:

In a food processor, blend herbs and garlic. Transfer to a jar with a lid and add vinegar to cover herbs. Seal jar tightly. Let it sit for one week in a cool dark place. After a week, add mustard powder, olive oil, garlic and horseradish to a food processor. Process to a smooth consistency. Store in a sealed container in the refrigerator. Using the optional horseradish sauce makes a spicy mustard.

BLOOD TYPE GROUPS:

Horseradish Salmon Salad Recipe

INGREDIENTS:

1 can of salmon

1/2 cup horseradish sauce

3 T chopped celery

1 T red onion (chopped)

1 T of vinegar

DIRECTIONS:

Combine salmon (with bones) in bowl with horseradish, celery, red onion and vinegar. Mix until smooth. Serve over salad.

BLOOD TYPE GROUPS:

Lemons & Limes

Lemon and Lime Fact Sheet

Beneficial to blood groups A and AB, and neutral to groups B and O, lemons are available year-round. The color and clearness of the skin is no clue to it's content. The skin texture is important: the thinner the skin the higher the juice content (also true for all citrus fruits). The smaller-sized lemons are normally thinner-skinned (thus higher in juice content). Rolling the lemon or lime with the palm of your hand on a hard surface or soaking for about 20 minutes in hot water will result in a higher juice yield.

Nutritional Data

- A single average lemon contains 16 milligrams of phosphorus, 2 milligrams of sodium, 26 grams of calcium, 138 grams of potassium, 53 milligrams of vitamin C and 0.6 grams of iron.

Therapeutic Benefits

- Straight fresh-squeezed lemon juice reduces fever. The minerals found in lemons help the formation of plasma, which are useful in treating the common cold, sore throat, cough and liver issues. Lemons act as an antiseptic to prevent infection, they also assist in cleansing the body of impurities. Lemons are a stimulant to the liver and a solvent for uric acids and other poisons. It liquifies bile; because of its potassium content it nourishes the brain and nerve cells. Containing calcium, it strengthens bone structure and produces healthy teeth.

Food Combining

- Lemons' medicinal properties outweigh its status as a fruit, thus is combinable with all food categories. Lemons can be squeezed on anything from fish to drinks.

At the Market

- Beneficial to blood group A and neutral to all others, Limes at their freshest will have a dark green tint to their skin; a yellowish lime is not fresh and will lack the necessary acidity that gives it flavor. As a lime ages further the skin will show brown scaled areas. Yellow or scaled limes can still be used; however, they will not be as potent as a dark green lime.

Lemon Custard Pudding Recipe

INGREDIENTS:

1 cup apple pectin (see Apple Peel Tea recipe, page 18)

6 lemons (squeeze and strain zest of 1/2)

1/2 cup agave (or to taste)

2 cups brown rice milk

DIRECTIONS:

Combine ingredients in a saucepan; bring to boil. Let simmer until desired thickness.

*Brown Rice Milk

Soak 1/2 lb brown rice overnight. Blend rice in blender and strain. Store remaining rice milk in refrigerator. Dehydrate the strained, gritty rice in oven on warm to be used later as a hot cereal replacement for cream of wheat.

BLOOD TYPE GROUPS:
A B
AB O

Dr. Peach's Lemon Slush Recipe

INGREDIENTS:

1 whole lemon cubed (maintaining seeds and skin)

Ice water

Maple syrup or blackstrap molasses

*The above item quantities vary based on personal preference.

DIRECTIONS:

Blend all ingredients together to the consistency of a drink or slush; serve hot or cold.

BLOOD TYPE GROUPS:
A B
AB O

Maple Syrup

Maple Syrup Fact Sheet

Neutral for all blood groups, pure maple syrup is a 100 percent natural food, processed by heat concentration of pure maple sap. This sap is a sterile, clear liquid, which provides the trees with water and nutrients prior to the buds and leaves opening in the spring. In the boiling, concentrating and filtering processes, all the nutrients remain in the syrup. There are some quantitative differences in maple syrup's nutritive composition due to metabolic and environmental differences among maple trees.

Nutritional Data

- Pure maple syrup is a good all-purpose sweetener. It is worth getting a good-quality maple syrup. Organic grade B does not contain chemical antifoamers, mold inhibitors and residues from formaldehyde pellets (commonly used to keep the tapped holes in the maple tree from healing). Maple syrup contains 60 percent vegetable sugar. Maple is a natural product and is not a raw food. Maple syrup contains significant amounts of calcium (20 mg/tbsp) and potassium (35 mg/tbsp), small amounts of iron and phosphorous, and trace amounts of B vitamins. Its sodium content is low (2 mg/tbsp).

Kitchen Tips

- Store maple syrup in your freezer to retain flavor and quality over an indefinite period of time. The syrup will not freeze solid and will require only about 1 hour at room temperature to bring it to pouring consistency. The amount required can be removed from the container, and the remainder may be returned to the freezer.

- If, after extended storage, mold should form on the surface of the syrup, the original quality can be restored. Remove the mold, heat the syrup to boiling, skim the surface, sterilize the container, and refill it with the syrup.

Maple Syrup Candy Recipe

INGREDIENTS:

2 cups pure maple syrup

Candy molds

Candy thermometer

DIRECTIONS:

Cook syrup in a saucepan over medium heat until it reaches 240° on a candy thermometer. Remove from heat and allow to cool to 200°. Stir constantly until syrup becomes sugary. Pour into molds (about the size of a caramel candy). When candy is cool, you can remove from molds. Makes about 16 candies.

BLOOD TYPE GROUPS:
A B
AB O

Peppermint Jubilee Recipe

INGREDIENTS:

64 ounces water

4 lemons

1/4 cup chlorophyll

1/4 cup maple syrup (or sweeten to taste)

6 peppermint tea bags

DIRECTIONS:

Bring water to a boil, add teabags and steep 5 minutes. Juice lemons. Combine all ingredients, blend, and add to a pitcher. This drink can be served hot or cold, depending on the time of year. It is very nutritious and refreshing.

Should you decide to make your own chlorophyll, simply blend a leafy green—like spinach, or even an herb like peppermint—in the blender with a small amount of water and strain.

BLOOD TYPE GROUPS:
A B
AB O

Nopales

Nopales Fact Sheet

[No Blood Group Data Available]

- Nopales is a prickly pear cactus that can be used to replace tomatoes. Tomatoes only combine with summer squash, eggplant and peppers, thus it becomes necessary for a replacement for the tomato, and nopales is it. Nopales can be eaten raw or cooked and taste like green beans.

Therapeutic Benefits

- Nopales is a wonderful vegetable—especially for diabetics because it balances blood sugar levels and lowers cholesterol. The sap in the pads can be used as a soup thickener, rubbed into the skin as a first-aid remedy like aloe vera, or as a mosquito repellent.

At the Market

- Select firm, evenly colored pads; store in a vegetable bin of the refrigerator. They will keep for 3 weeks.

Kitchen Tips

- To prepare the pad, simply hold its base and scrape the skin on both sides with a blunt knife until all the spines are removed. Then peel the pads and cut them into shoestring strips or dice them according to the needs of the recipe. They can be eaten raw in salads, boiled, sautéed or pickled with spices.

Sweet and Sour Sauce Recipe

INGREDIENTS:

1/4 cup nopales
1/4 cup liquid amino
1/4 cup lemon juice or apple cider vinegar (optional)
2 t agave
1 cup water

DIRECTIONS:

Combine ingredients and heat to simmer. Turn off heat and serve.

BLOOD TYPE GROUPS:

Salsa Recipe

INGREDIENTS:

1/4 cup Nopales

1/8 cup olive oil

1 red bell pepper (optional)

1 fresh lime or lemon (juiced)

3 cloves garlic

15 sprigs of cilantro

1 jalapeño

3 green onions

Ginger slice (quarter-sized)

DIRECTIONS:

Slice jalapeño into quarters. Keep 1/4 slice of seeds. Remove seed and pith of the remaining 3/4. Chop and place all of the ingredients into a food processor and process to desired texture. Note that there are no seasonings present in this recipe; this is done for optimal health.

BLOOD TYPE GROUPS:

Onion

Onion Fact Sheet

Beneficial for blood groups A and O, and neutral to AB and B, onions are nature's cure-all. Evidence from studies indicate that eating raw onions may help to reduce abnormally high cholesterol levels and combat harmful effects that eating fatty foods can have on the blood. Experts think that the sulphur compounds that onions contain may possibly help to prevent the growth of cancer cells. (It is this compound that gives onions this flavor and strong smell.)

Nutritional Data

- In looking for the nutrients that are present in onions, our attention should not be focused so much on their vitamin content, as on their incredibly rich trace element content. Garlic and onion contain 3 very important minerals: normally sulphur, potassium, and germanium in that order.

Therapeutic Benefits

- Intestinal parasites thrive in the gut and colon of many human beings. Raw garlic and onion therapy has been extremely beneficial in removing these worms. The strong sulphur in both culinary herbs overwhelm the parasites—knocking them into a stupor via their vapors or immobilizing them by "poisoning" the circulating blood plasma around them, from which they derive their nourishment. While in such temporary paralysis, they are no longer able to cling to intestinal wall tissue, thereby enabling the body to throw them off in normal bowel movements.

At the Market

- A great onion is firm, dry and well-shaped, with a sweet aroma and no sprouts.

Kitchen Tips

- Store whole onions in a cool dry place with good ventilation—not in the refrigerator. Scallions and cut onions, however, should be wrapped tightly in plastic wrap and refrigerated.

- How to cook: Onion skin is one of the best sources of the compound guercetin, reported to decrease capillary fragility. To get the full benefits of the guercetin, cook the whole unpeeled onion whenever possible and discard the skin before serving.

Roasted Stuffed Onion Recipe

INGREDIENTS:

1 large onion for each person

4 cups cooked black beans (or bean of choice)

1/2 cup almond cheese

2 salmon chorizos (or 2 cups fish of choice)

*add optional salsa (see Salsa Recipe, page 85)

DIRECTIONS:

Cut 1/3 of the top across the onion like a hat. Cut off bottoms so that onions can sit flat. Scoop out large inner areas leaving 3 or 4 layers of onion skin. Preheat oven to 350°. In a pan with just enough water to cover the bottom, place scooped-out onions and chorizo or fish and cook until tender. Afterwards, add black beans and cheese to fish combination and fill the hulled onions with the mixture. Bake in oven for 25 minutes or until tender. Serve.

BLOOD TYPE GROUPS:
A B
AB O

Onion Soup Recipe

INGREDIENTS:

8 large onions

3 T olive oil

2 stalks of celery

3 cloves of garlic

3 T vegetarian Worcestershire sauce (optional)

3 T liquid amino or to taste (optional)

DIRECTIONS:

Finely chop celery. Mince garlic cloves. Slice onions. Sauté onions, celery and garlic until translucent, in a stock pot, adding a little water to keep from sticking. Add onion sauté, until onions begin to brown; add hot vegetable stock until onions are covered by liquid. Simmer 15 minutes. Stir in Worcestershire sauce and liquid amino. Serve.

BLOOD TYPE GROUPS:
A B
AB O

Pear

Pear Fact Sheet

Neutral for all blood groups, pears are a useful source of fiber and potassium. Pears are among the least allergenic of foods.

Nutritional Data

- Tree fruits contain vitamins A and C and are rich in minerals such as magnesium and calcium. Fruits may be combined with other fruits without qualms. It is not necessary to take the acid or sugar content into account at all, with the exception of rhubarbs, which contain so much oxalic acid it is better to be avoided and its leaves are particularly toxic and should never be eaten.

- Acid fruits may be combined with fatty foods such as goat cheese and almonds.

- A simple pear has a total fiber content of 5 grams, which is quite a bit. Four grams of this is the soluble kind with special benefits to digestive health.

Therapeutic Benefits

- Pears are one of the better sources of caffeic and chlorogenic acids. Caffeic acid is an immune stimulate, and researchers have found chlorogenic works against HIV, herpes, and shingles—in fresh juice or preserved pear form.

- Pears and pear juices have a decidedly cooling effect upon the septum in cases of mild to extreme fevers. In fact, when no other type of nourishment can be tolerated by the stomach, either of these is neutral enough to be eaten with good success.

- Indigestion: Where an acidic condition may prevail in the gut due to heavy consumption of greasy or spicy foods, or simply just from overeating—a cup of pear juice, slowly sipped, will help relieve some of the intestinal discomforts.

At the Market

- Look for pears that are light green to gold in color, with a bit of pink. Surface blemishes make a less attractive pear; however they do not affect the quality.

Kitchen Tips

- Store pears at room temperature until ripe. Store in a loosely closed brown paper bag. Group several together at a time because they release gases that help the others ripen. Anjin pears, unlike others, will ripen in the refrigerator. Pears ripen from the inside out—if they become too soft on the outside, they may be mushy inside.

- Pears should be eaten when the aromatic necks give a little when touched. Eat immediately or refrigerate up to 4 days.

Pears with Goat Cheese Recipe (appetizer)

INGREDIENTS:

2 ripe, medium-sized pears

5 ounces goat cheese

Fresh mint leaves

DIRECTIONS:

Peel pears. Remove and discard the cores. Divide the cheese slices and garnish with mint leaves.

BLOOD TYPE
GROUPS:

Baked Pears Recipe

INGREDIENTS:

1/3 cup dates

1/4 cup almonds

2 cups goat gouda

4 peeled pears (halved and cored)

1 cup of apple or pear juice

DIRECTIONS:

Preheat oven to 350°. Combine dates and almonds in a food processor or blender and process until finely chopped. Add cheese and continue to process until a soft ball forms. Spoon the cheese mixture into the cavity of pears and set them in a casserole dish. Pour the juice around them. Bake until the pears are tender (about 35 minutes). Serve hot.

Makes 4 servings.

BLOOD TYPE
GROUPS:

Pear Ginger Sauce Recipe

INGREDIENTS:

8 fresh pears (peeled and diced)

1 1/2 cups water

1/4 cups fresh ginger juice

2 juiced lemons

6 dates

DIRECTIONS:

Cover dates with water and soak them overnight. Remove seeds from dates and chop them. In a pan, simmer all ingredients until soft. Serve.

BLOOD TYPE
GROUPS:
A B
AB 0

Pear Supreme Recipe

INGREDIENTS:

1/2 cup of almonds (chopped)

1 1/2 tablespoon of olive oil

2 teaspoons of freshly squeezed lemon juice

1/4 cup of date sugar

2 firm pears (skin on; halved, cored and cut lengthwise into a minimum of 16 slices, 1/16-inch thick, tossed with 2 teaspoons of freshly-squeezed lemon juice)

2 ripe pears (peeled, halved, cored and cut into small wedges, tossed in olive oil)

DIRECTIONS:

In the center of each plate, place small pear wedges tossed in olive oil. Scoop three tablespoons of warm pear ginger sauce on top and sprinkle with date sugar; arrange firm pear slices on the top and sprinkle with chopped almonds.

BLOOD TYPE
GROUPS:
A B
AB 0

Pepper

Peppers Fact Sheet

Peppers are beneficial for blood group B, neutral for O, and should be avoided by groups AB and A. Red bell peppers are an important source of vitamin C. Green bell peppers are not ripe. Bell peppers contain useful amounts of beta-carotene and bioflavonoids. Chilies are rich in vitamin C. Red bell peppers contain up to three times the vitamin C as an orange.

• The fierce heat of chilies comes from the capsaicin in their white ribs, flesh and seeds.

• Bell peppers rate among the most nutrient-dense foods. Nutrient-dense means the amount of nutrition food delivers for each calorie it provides.

• According to calculations by the Basic and Traditional Foods Association, various kinds of green and red bell peppers are rated amongst the highest nutrient-dense foods.

Therapeutic Benefits

• Chilies can relieve congestion in blocked airways and are thought to have anticoagulant and cholesterol-lowering properties.

At the Market

• Select sweet bell peppers that have firm walls and are a heavy and full size. Many peppers start green, turning red, yellow or purple upon maturing.

Kitchen Tips

• Store peppers in tightly closed plastic bags in the crisper drawer of the refrigerator. They will last up to 2 weeks.

Stuffed Peppers Recipe

INGREDIENTS:

6 bell peppers (red, yellow or orange)

3 cups Jasmine rice (cooked)

1/4 cup red onion (diced)

1/4 cup celery (diced)

1/4 cup zucchini (diced)

1/4 cup broccoli (finely chopped)

4 cloves of garlic (finely chopped)

1/2 T granulated garlic

1/2 T paprika

1/4 t turmeric

DIRECTIONS:

Core and cut bell peppers in half. Broil peppers in the oven with outer side towards broiler. Sauté vegetables in a skillet until translucent (shiny). Add rice and seasoning; mix ingredients thoroughly. Place sautéed vegetables and rice in bell pepper halves and bake in the oven at 250° for 15 minutes. Serve.

Different varieties of vegetables can be substituted.

BLOOD TYPE GROUPS:
B   O

Jalapeño Seasoning Recipe

INGREDIENTS:

1 dozen jalapeños

6 red, yellow, orange and green bell peppers (optional)

2 lemons

DIRECTIONS:

Quarter jalapeños, place on baking sheet, Dehydrate in the oven on warm until dry. Once dry, grind into powder in a food processor. Seasoning can be used to spice up soups, salads and other dishes.

Taking the pith and seeds out will produce a milder seasoning. The heat in peppers is contained in the pith (white part) and the seeds.

Dehydrate your favorite pepper to add zest and flavor to your dishes. Red, yellow, orange and green bell peppers make an excellent seasoning. If you find you have peppers that are starting to break down, just dehydrate them.

Grate the skin off lemons that you have juiced and dehydrate and mix with pepper seasoning to make lemon pepper, or use the dehydrated lemon for lemon zest. It is used in baking and added to teas when you are out of lemon.

BLOOD TYPE GROUPS:
B   O

Pineapple Fact Sheet

Beneficial for blood groups A, AB and B, and neutral for group O, pineapples pack power. Traditionally pineapple has been thought to possess various healing powers, but modern nutritional science has concentrated on the fact that the fruit contains a powerful enzyme called bromelain, which acts to break down protein. Researchers believe that the substance may help to break up blood clots, and there is scientific evidence to suggest that it may help to relieve congested sinuses. Bromelain is thought to speed the repair of damaged tissues, so it is used to treat arthritis. Herbal practitioners advise gargling with the juice to relieve a sore throat and eating pineapple as a treatment of various disorders, including catarrh, bronchitis and indigestion. There are 1,500 species in 65 general categories in the bromeliaceal or pineapple family.

Additional Blood Group Information for Pineapple Enzyme (Bromelain)

Blood groups specific beneficial effect :
- All blood groups—allergy control, anti-inflammation and surgery recovery.
- Group A—antibiotic support
- Group O—urinary tract health

Nutritional Data

- One slice of raw pineapple contains the following nutrients:
  14 mg calcium, 7 mg phosphorus, 0.4 mg iron, 1 mg sodium, 123 mg potassium, 60 I.U., vitamin C, 34 mg magnesium and small amounts of vitamin E.

Therapeutic Benefits

- Bromelian is an anti-inflammatory agent used to treat minor injuries, particularly sprains, strains, muscle injuries and the pain, swelling and tenderness that accompanies sports injuries. Bromelian is also good for angina, asthma, minor injuries and urinary tract infections.

- In rare instances, fresh pineapples may trigger allergic reactions. Also, those suffering from diabetes and hypoglycemia should exercise caution with pineapple intake.

At the Market

- Unlike other fruit, pineapples do not become sweeter after they are picked. To see if a pineapple is ripe, hold it and check its leaves for color. The fruit should feel heavy for its size, the leaves should be fresh and green, and the pineapple should smell sweet and fragrant. Always eat fresh pineapple as opposed to canned, because the canning process destroys the bromelain.

Lovely Tropical Pineapple Jam Recipe

INGREDIENTS:

2 ripe pineapples

2 limes

Date sugar (the same amount as the weight of the fruit)

DIRECTIONS:

Slice the tops off the pineapples then cut off the peel in strips, cutting deep enough to remove the "eyes." Cut the pineapples into thick slices; cut out and throw away the hard core and dice the remaining flesh. Weigh the fruit. Add the same weight in date sugar. Put fruit into a saucepan. Warm the date sugar. Allow 1 lime for each 450g fruit. Peel the zest and finely slice. Halve and squeeze the limes, keeping the juice. Roughly chop the lime halves. Put them on a square of tightly woven cheese-cloth and tie up tightly in a bag with a long piece of string. Put the lime zest and juice into the pan with the pineapple and tie the muslin bag string to the pan handle. Stir over low heat until the sugar has dissolved. Increase the heat and bring to a boil, then simmer, stirring occasionally for about 90 minutes. Remove the pan from the heat. Test for set. Discard the bag, squeezing it first to extract all the juice. Lightly skim off any scum using a long-handled metal spoon. Immediately pour the jam into warmed sterilized jars, within 3 mm of the top. Seal the jars and label.

BLOOD TYPE GROUPS:

A B

AB O

Grilled Pineapple Slices Recipe

INGREDIENTS:

1 ripe pineapple

DIRECTIONS:

Core the pineapple and slice 1/2-inch thick. Place slices on grill or in skillet on medium heat. Remove pineapple slices from grill when they begin to blacken.

Serve warm.

BLOOD TYPE GROUPS:

A B

AB O

Rice

Rice Fact Sheet

Neutral for groups A, B and O, and beneficial for AB blood groups. Rice is a source of starch and gluten–free carbohydrates. Most of its nutrients are contained in the bran and the germ. Brown rice varieties are more nutritious on the whole than white ones. Eating too much white rice can lead to a lack of thiamine in the body, while too much brown rice can result in iron and calcium deficiencies.

- Brown rice in particular is an excellent source of dietary fiber. All rice has the added health benefit of being easily digestible.

Varieties of Rice

- Basmati—a long-grain aromatic
- Jasmine—fragrant rice
- Wild rice—is not classified botanically as a true rice; it is the seed of a wild aquatic grass in North America

Therapeutic Benefits

- Rice benefits: on its own, rice is easily digestible. In health terms, it is a good source of complex carbohydrates, which are digested and absorbed slowly, releasing glucose into the bloodstream steadily rather than in a massive spurt. This makes blood sugar levels easier to stabilize and control. Rice is also gluten–free and ideal for people with gluten intolerance.
- Rice is the staple food of half the world. It is packed with useful starches, B vitamins, calcium and iron.

At the Market

- Long-grain rice, when cooked, becomes separate and light grey. Medium-grain is plumper and starchier than long-grain. Short grain is very starchy and heavy.
- To determine freshness, smell the rice. If there is any trace of mustiness or rancidity, do not purchase.

Kitchen Tips

- Store rice in tightly covered glass jars in the refrigerator; it will last up to 6 months.
- To reheat refrigerated rice, scoop it into a mesh strainer and steam over boiling water until heated through.
- Before cooking the rice, wash 2-3 times in a mesh strainer to remove excess starch.

Rice Milk Recipe

INGREDIENTS:

1 gallon of water

1/2 lb rice

DIRECTIONS:

Soak rice overnight. Blend rice in blender; then strain. Store remaining rice milk in the refrigerator. Dehydrate the strained, gritty rice in an oven on warm to be used later as a hot cereal replacement for cream of wheat.

BLOOD TYPE
GROUPS:

A B
AB O

Spring Rolls Recipe

INGREDIENTS:

12 (8-inch) round sheets of rice paper

3 large carrots

2 zucchini

3 cups bean sprouts

3 green onions

1 red bell pepper (optional)

1 yellow bell pepper (optional)

DIRECTIONS:

Cut carrots, zucchini and bell peppers into 2-inch julienne slices. Slice green onion lengthwise into slivers 2 inches long.

Steam carrots, zucchini, bean sprouts and bell peppers for 3 minutes. Add hot water to a large shallow dish to the depth of 1 inch. Place rice paper wrapper sheet in hot water dish for 30-45 seconds. Place soaked sheet of rice on a plate. Place and stack strips of carrot, zucchini, bell pepper, bean sprout and green onion in the center of the rice paper roll. Fold sides and roll up in jelly roll fashion. Place in covered container until ready to serve.

BLOOD TYPE
GROUPS:

A B
AB O

Salmon Fact Sheet

Beneficial for blood groups A, B and AB, also neutral to group O, salmon offers heart health benefits. Research at the University of Land in Sweden shows that salmon benefits the Heart by making the blood less prone to the abnormal clotting process that can lead to a heart attack. The Omega-3 fats in fish are credited with this effect. Three-and-one-half ounces of raw or canned salmon contain 1.7 grams of Omega-3 fatty acid.

Therapeutic Benefits

- With generous amounts of potassium and only modest amounts of sodium, salmon rates high for keeping blood pressure in the healthy range. Use unsalted seasonings to keep sodium content at the moderate level that nature put there.

- Yasuo Kagowa and co-workers at Gichi Medical School in Japan have shown that levels of the "good" HDL cholesterol are highest among the Japanese who eat the most fish. A research team at The University of Oregon has documented a dramatic effect of a diet rich in sodium oil. Ten days on the diet lowered blood cholesterol by as much as 20 percent and cut blood triglycerides by as much as 40-67 percent.

- In the *Eat Right for Your Blood Type Encyclopedia*, fish oils are listed as having anti-inflammation properties for treatment of arthritis and blood thinners used to treat Crohn's Disease, high blood pressure, high triglycerides and rheumatoid arthritis. This book also lists salmon as a nutrient-dense food containing components that positively influence known disease susceptibility.

At the Market

- Canned fish is now available in low-sodium and water-packed varieties.

Kitchen Tips

- To store fresh fish, wrap in wax paper and keep in the coldest part of the refrigerator for up to 2 days. If you need to keep it longer, wrap in foil or freezer bags and freeze. Most fish will keep frozen from 3-6 months. Leftovers from an opened can of fish may be transferred onto a non-metal container and stored in the refrigerator. It should remain tasty for up to a week.

- To remove some of the sodium content from salted canned salmon, rinse under cool water for 30 seconds. Pat dry before using.

Salmon Bacon Recipe

INGREDIENTS:

1 lb. thinly-sliced salmon filet (lateral or vertical slice)

4 T of liquid amino

5 T of Liquid Smoke®

DIRECTIONS:

Combine liquid amino and Liquid Smoke® to make a marinade. Marinade bacon at least one hour on each side. For best results, marinade overnight. Broil on cookie sheet until crispy.

FOR SALMON JERKY

After marinating, roll filet flat with a pastry rolling pin. Dehydrate in oven at 120° over night or until thoroughly dry in oven.

BLOOD TYPE GROUPS:
A B
AB O

Salmon Spread Recipe

INGREDIENTS:

1 14-oz. can salmon (Red Sockeye®)

2 cloves of garlic

1 t capers (drained)

2 T lemon juice

2 T eggless mayo

1/2 t paprika

DIRECTIONS:

Drain salmon and remove skin. Put all ingredients into a food processor. Blend ingredients until smooth, adding more eggless mayo if necessary. Chill up to 24 hours and serve.

Makes approx. 1 1/2 cups.

*Hand Method: Combine ingredients in a medium bowl and mash with a potato masher until thoroughly combined.

BLOOD TYPE GROUPS:
A B
AB O

Squash

Squash Fact Sheet

Neutral for all blood groups, squash is a good source of beta-carotene; it also provides the body with useful amounts of vitamin E. The seeds are rich in iron, magnesium, phosphorus, potassium and zinc. Large zucchini seeds have been used in folk medicine for centuries as a diuretic and as part of a treatment for tapeworms. Most of the nutrient content is contained in the vegetable's skin.

• In food combining, squash combines with both protein and starch.

Therapeutic Benefits

• With very low levels of fat and sodium, squash are also ideal for heart-healthy diets. A cup of acorn squash has almost 100 milligrams of calcium.

• Yellow squash and zucchini help with controlling blood pressure and weight. Winter squash has nutritional density.

At the Market

• Squash should have a hard rind and feel heavy for its size. Picking ones that still have stems will help you avoid ones that are rotted inside.

• All squash should be free of gashes, mold, or soft spots.

Kitchen Tips

• Store squash in a cool, dry place with good circulation. If conditions are good, it may last all winter. About 55° is ideal; colder temperatures are not advised.

• In a conventional oven set at 400°, halved squash will bake in about 35 minutes.

Spaghetti Squash Recipe

INGREDIENTS:

2 medium spaghetti squash

Sweet-and-Sour sauce (see page 85)

chopped vegetables of choice

DIRECTIONS:

Cut spaghetti squash in half and remove seeds. Bake face down in lightly oiled baking dish for 30-45 minutes, depending on the size. When properly cooked, the spaghetti squash will scrape out of the squash halves in strands. If cooked too long, it will get mushy. Scrape squash onto plate with fork. Top with sauce.

Sauce:

Sauté desired vegetables in garlic, thyme, marjoram seasonings. And add a little hot water to keep from sticking. Serve with spelt garlic bread. Use fresh basil and fresh garlic if available. Excellent in marinara sauce, spaghetti squash can also be served with salmon balls. Use 4 cans of salmon, season with dry Italian seasoning, basil, liquid amino and garlic. Shape into jaw breaker-sized balls, then cook in an oven on a lightly greased sheet. Season with Liquid Smoke®, fresh sage and fennel seed. Add beet juice to the sauce if you would like it to be red.

BLOOD TYPE GROUPS:

A B
AB O

Spicy Squash Recipe

INGREDIENTS:

1 large butternut squash

1/4 t ground mace

1/4 t ground allspice

Seeds of 2 cardamom pods (ground)

1 T maple syrup

2 t olive oil

DIRECTIONS:

Cut squash in half, then scrape out and discard the seeds (or save seeds for roasting). Slice squash into manageable chunks (about 1-2 inches) and boil in enough water to cover until tender (about 20 minutes).

When squash is cool enough to handle, remove the skin and spoon flesh into a food processor or blender. Add mace, allspice, ground cardamom seeds, maple syrup and olive oil. Process until smooth.

Serve hot as a side dish. Makes 4 servings.

BLOOD TYPE GROUPS:

A B
AB O

Squash Burgers Recipe

INGREDIENTS:

1 cup butternut squash (steamed)

1 cup rice (cooked)

1 t of sage

Pinch of thyme

Pinch of spike

2 T Italian seasonings

Sprouted or spelt bread crumbs

DIRECTIONS:

Toast bread and grind in a food processor with Italian seasonings. Mash the first 5 ingredients together. Form into balls; roll balls in bread crumb mixture. Flatten into patties. Bake at 400° for 50 minutes.

BLOOD TYPE GROUPS:

A B
AB O

Zucchini Boats Recipe

INGREDIENTS:

4 zucchini

1-cup sliced tomatoes (any variety)

1 sprig of thyme

1 sprig of rosemary

1 basil leaf

1 pinch of Italian seasoning

DIRECTIONS:

Cut stem off zucchini and slice lengthwise. Use a knife and slice indentation in the center of the zucchini. Scoop out seeded portion of zucchini, dice scooped out zucchini and sauté in pan with tomatoes, herbs and seasoning. Season and broil zucchini hulls for 4-6 minutes. Add filling to hulls.

BLOOD TYPE GROUPS:

A B
O

Zucchini Parmesan Recipe

INGREDIENTS:

3 zucchinis (medium to large)

2 yellow squash

3 T nutritional yeast

2 32-oz. cans of diced tomatoes

1 can tomato paste

2 medium onions (diced)

2 stalks celery

1 bell pepper (optional)

6 cloves garlic (minced)

One bunch fresh basil

Dry Italian seasoning or pizza seasoning sauce

DIRECTIONS:

Sauté the onions, celery, bell pepper and garlic. Add diced tomatoes and tomato paste. Simmer on stove 2 hours after bringing to a boil. Chop and add basil the last 10 minutes.

Slice zucchini 1/4-inch thick. Lightly oil a Pyrex pan. Spread zucchini slices in pan, then add a layer of sauce and sprinkle nutritional yeast over the top. Repeat this process as often as ingredients will allow. As a finishing touch, an optional top layer of rice cheese or goat cheese may be added.

BLOOD TYPE GROUPS:

O

Transitional Recipes for Food Combining & Blood Typing

Zucchini Delight Recipe

INGREDIENTS:

3 large red, yellow, or orange peppers (optional)

3 medium-sized zucchinis

10 medium-sized ripe tomatoes

1/2 green chili pepper (optional)

A pinch of dried oregano

A pinch of dried basil

DIRECTIONS:

Rinse, dry and coarsely chop chili peppers and red, yellow or orange peppers. Dice zucchini. Blanch, peel and seed the tomatoes and chop coarsely. Use drained, canned tomatoes if necessary. In a cast iron skillet, add 1/2 cup of water. When this gets very hot, add the peppers, chili peppers and zucchini. Stir well and season to taste. Cover and reduce heat to low. Simmer gently for 25 minutes, stirring occasionally.

Mix chopped tomato flesh with oregano and basil in a small saucepan. Bring to a boil, stirring occasionally. Simmer uncovered for about 10 minutes, stirring frequently as the sauce reduces and thickens considerably. When it is very thick, stir in the pepper mixture and cook over low heat until thick. Serve when ready.

BLOOD TYPE GROUPS:

O

Transitional Recipes for Food Combining & Blood Typing

Spelt

Spelt Fact Sheet

Neutral for all blood groups, spelt is one of the first grains to be grown by early farmers as long ago as 5,000 B.C., and is finding renewed popularity with American consumers.

- Spelt's "nutty" flavor has long been popular in Europe, where it is also known as "Farro" (Italy) and "Dinkle" (Germany). In Roman times it was "Farrum," and origins can be traced back to early Mesopotamia. Spelt (triticum spelta) is an ancient and distant cousin to modern wheat (Triticum aestivum). Spelt is one of the oldest of cultivated grains, preceded only by Emmer and Elkorn.

Nutritional Data

- The grain is naturally high in fiber. Spelt is also high in B-complex vitamins, and both simple and complex carbohydrates. Another important benefit is that some gluten-sensitive people have been able to include spelt-based foods in their diets.

- Spelt's uniqueness is also derived from its genetic makeup and nutrition profile. Total protein content is from 10-25 percent greater than the common varieties of commercial wheat.

- Spelt has a tough hull, or husk, that makes it more difficult to process than modern wheat varieties. However, the husk, separated just before milling, not only protects the kernel but helps retain nutrients and maintain freshness. Modern wheat has changed dramatically over the decades, as it has been bred to be easier to grow and harvest, to increase yield, and to have a high gluten content for the production of high-volume commercial baked goods. Unlike wheat, spelt has retained many of its original traits and remains highly nutritious and full of flavor.

- Also, unlike other grains, spelt's husk protects it from pollutants and insects and usually allows growers to avoid using pesticides.

- Since its reintroduction to the market in 1987 by Purity Foods Inc., spelt has become a top-selling product in the organic and health food markets. Flour made from the versatile grain can be substituted for wheat flour in breads, pasta, cookies, crackers, cakes, muffins, pancakes and waffles.

Therapeutic Benefits

- Spelt has high water solubility, so the nutrients are easily absorbed by the body. Spelt contains special carbohydrates which are an important factor in blood clotting and stimulating the body's immune system. It is also a superb fiber resource and has large amounts of B-complex vitamins.

[continued on next page]

More Than Superior Taste

• Spelt is more than just a nutritious product. The whole grain flour is the perfect answer for those people who want to eat good, tasty whole-grain products. Organic, unbleached spelt flour is the same grain with most of the bran (fiber) removed, and nothing added.

Ancient Grain with Modern Day Appeal

• Not to be confused with oats or wheat, spelt is a member of the same grain family but is an entirely different species. It is one of the original seven grains mentioned in the Bible. This 9000-year-old grain originated in the Fertile Crescent and over the centuries found its way throughout Europe, where it remained a very popular grain for hundreds of years.

Delicate Kernel Is the Secret

• The secret to spelt's mild flavor and superior performance can be attributed to the tough outer hull protecting the spelt kernel. Unlike common wheat, which loses its hull when harvested, spelt kernels have to be transported to a custom processing center to dehull and clean the grain. It is believed that the impervious outer hull allows for the development of a more delicate, water-soluble kernel. It also protects the grain from pollutants and insects and enhances the retention of the nutrients in the kernel and improves freshness.

Spelt Bread Recipe

INGREDIENTS:

2 cups spelt flour

1 pack of quick-rising dry yeast

2 T of maple sugar sweetener

Pinch of salt

2/3 cup very warm almond or rice milk

2 T olive oil

DIRECTIONS:

In large bowl, combine flour, yeast, maple sugar and salt. Stir in almond or rice milk and 1 tablespoon of olive oil until dough forms. Turn dough out onto floured board and knead about 3 minutes, or until smooth. Grease mixing bowl and place dough in bowl, turning to coat lightly. Cover and place in a warm spot away from drafts. Let rise about 30 minutes.

Heat oven to 350°. Place dough on greased baking sheet, or, if desired, bake in greased 8x4-inch loaf pan. Brush with remaining tablespoon of olive oil and bake about 25 minutes or until golden and loaf sounds hollow when tapped on top.

BLOOD TYPE GROUPS:

Spelt Eggless Roll Wrappers Recipe

INGREDIENTS:

2 cups spelt flour (white or whole; or use one cup of each)

1/2 cup ice water

1 T of liquid lecithin

DIRECTIONS:

Combine ingredients. Kneed for 5 minutes. Cover and let stand for 30 minutes. Divide into small 1/2-inch diameter balls. Roll out onto plastic wrap paper. Fill with sautéed vegetables of your choice.

BLOOD TYPE GROUPS:

Sprouted Bread Fact Sheet

Bread is referred to as the staff of life, yet, in most cases it is one of the most denatured foods consumed. Bread is a denatured food because after the grain has been cultivated, the grain is left to die and dry out. From there it is stripped of its germ and bran. Then it is pulverized into a grain that is stored in a silo. Because of the infestation of rodents, bugs, and other pests, the germ is brominated (meaning poisoned to kill the pests). Next, the dry, dead grain—with poison and pest parts—are again pulverized (milled) into flour (a nutritionally devoid powder), which in turn is further processed into bread.

- Any common supermarket store bread is made with so many chemicals and preservatives you need a Ph.D. to understand the ingredients. For example, one of the ingredients most often found in commercial bread is mono-diglycerides; this is a term used to deceive consumers from the fact that this ingredient is derived from animal byproducts such as swine. A bread without preservatives, unless refrigerated, will begin to mold within a matter of days. Commercial bread is so dead that it takes weeks for it to mold.

- Commercial bread is dead because it has no natural nutrients. There are whole wheat breads on the market, however they are subject to storage and spoilage problems. Once the wheat has been stripped of its bran and germ, nothing of nutritional value remains. The germ is removed because it contains live nutrients that spoil quickly. The germ of the wheat has live proteins, vitamins E and B-complex, and essential fatty acids. Most B vitamins and essential fats are sensitive to heat, light and air. Once exposed to the high baking temperature and left at room temperature, the wheat germ becomes rancid within 24-48 hours. Rancidity is the process where essential fatty acids deteriorate into peroxides and aldehydes that are known to cause cancer and disease in the intestinal tracts.

- Wheat is also one of the most allergy-producing foods consumed. Wheat has gluten–a gluey protein that is responsible for the bread dough's cohesiveness. It is very bad for digestion. Gluten is so sticky that it is the major ingredient in wallpaper paste. Gluten is the primary allergic factor in wheat. Undigested proteins irritate and cause allergic reactions to occur.

  Let's consider how partially digestible bread is consumed. The most popular way bread is eaten is via the sandwich. Bread is a carbohydrate. Carbohydrates/grains do not combine with proteins because they digest at different rates. Thus ,you are left with partially-digested food in the colon that becomes putrid.

Now that we have looked at the problem, let's address the solution. Because we have become accustomed to eating bread we need to find an alternative bread that will digest and has nutrients. This bread is sprouted bread. Sprouted bread is far more nutritious than traditional bread and easily digested. During the process of spouting, complex starches are simplified into sugars producing a byproduct known as maltose. Maltose gives sprouted breads sweetness so there is no need for sweeteners. Also, making sprouted bread does not require yeast, salt, or baking powder. There is a synergetic process that takes place with sprouted breads. New protein from building blocks of starch, sugars and fats—within the germinating seed—undergo an increase in amino acids. During germination the difficult-to-digest gluten breaks down and the mineral-binding acids such as oxalic and phytic acids are also destroyed. With germination, enzyme levels are elevated, amylase initiates the breakdown of starches and protease initiates the breakdown of protein, invertase of sugar and lipase of fats. Thus sprouted bread is more easily digested.

Sprouted Bread Recipe

There are four simple steps in making sprouted bread (use a grain that is neutral for your blood type):

Step 1: Grow the sprouts. The best and easiest way to grow sprouts is with a sprouting bag. Soak your seeds in a jar for 12-15 hours. Then sprout them for 2 days in a sprout bag. Dip the bag twice a day to rinse.

Step 2: Grind the sprouts into a smooth paste. When the tail of the sprout is the same length as the seed, they are ready to grind. Let your sprouts dry 3-6 hours before grinding them. The grinding of sprouts can be achieved with a food processor, a juicer that can function as a grinder, a wheatgrass juicer or meat grinder. Blenders do not work because they liquefy.

Step 3: Make the loaves. Kneading is not necessary; however, the more you knead the more cohesive the dough becomes and the more it will rise. Form a ball of dough about 3 inches in diameter and place on a baking tray.

Step 4: Bake and store. Pre-heat your oven to 250°. The bread should be done in 2 1/2-3 1/2 hours. Sprouted bread keeps for two weeks in the refrigerator or may be frozen for longer storage.

Sprouted breads are available commercially at health food stores. They are a much healthier alternative to denatured flour breads. You will find them in the frozen food section of the store. Some of the sprouted breads are similar to the flour breads in that they contain yeast. Even still they are much better for you than flour breads. Also available are sprouted flat breads or wraps that you can use to replace flour tortillas.

BLOOD TYPE
GROUPS:
A B
AB O

Tostada Recipe

The large sprouted wraps can be formed into a bowl to make tostadas. Place the wrap in a saucepan shaping them into a tostada bowl. Bake in the oven on low or warm for 10 minutes or to desired crispness.

You may use a glass or stainless steel sauce pan to form sprouted wrap bowls. The bowls hold their shape even after adding ingredients.

Tostada ingredients can be made to conform with a variety of blood types. For instance; navy beans for AB and B blood types, black beans for A and O blood types—or you can use small white beans or northern beans, which are indicated for all blood types. Canned or fresh salmon are another alternative. You are free to be creative with the tostada bowls.

The small-sized sprouted wraps can be shaped into taco shells. This taco is filled with refried beans, lettuce, rice cheese and topped with Veganaise®. Another variation would be to sauté canned salmon with taco seasoning, lettuce, nutritional yeast and top with Veganaise®.

BLOOD TYPE
GROUPS:
A B
AB O

Mini Pizza Recipe

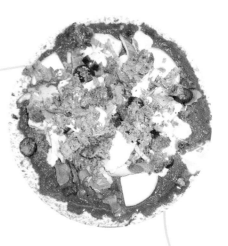

INGREDIENTS:

Sauce:

1 medium beet

4 carrots

1 medium onion

3 stalks celery

4 cloves garlic

1 T each of basil, oregano, thyme, marjoram, or optional seasoning (dulse, spike, liquid amino, kelp).

DIRECTIONS:

Roast vegetables, blend, add seasoning, simmer in saucepan for 20 minutes.

Use sprouted bread wraps as the crust. Spread sauce. Add topping, broil in oven 5-8 minutes.

Pizza toppings:

Make your pizza toppings blood-type correct and properly food-combined. For instance: if you decide to put salmon on the pizza and would like to have cheese, you would use almond cheese; if you use vegetables, you may use rice cheese, and nutritional yeast can be used in place of cheese.

BLOOD TYPE GROUPS:

A   B

AB   O

Sprouted Wrap Sandwiches Recipe

INGREDIENTS:

10 sprouted wraps

1 pack of cheddar rice cheese

1 pack of jalapeño rice cheese

1 pack of fresh spinach

3 large onions (sautéed)

3 peppers assorted colors (red, yellow, green, orange, sauteed—optional)

3/4 cup Veganaise®

1 pack of fresh sprouts of your choice

DIRECTIONS:

Warm wraps, spread 1 tablespoon of Veganaise® on wraps. Add several leaves of fresh spinach then 2 slices of cheese, one of each type. Top with sautéed onions and peppers. Roll into wrap and enjoy.

BLOOD TYPE GROUPS:

A   B

AB   O

Tomato

Tomato Fact Sheet

Neutral for blood groups AB and O, and should be avoided by groups B and A, vine-ripened tomatoes contain 23 calories per 2 1/2-inch tomato. Tomatoes are a member of the potato family; their beta-carotene, vitamin E and lycopene (the pigment that colors the skin as they ripen) reduces the chances of free radicals damaging the body.

Therapeutic Benefits

• Chronic Fatigue Syndrome, fatigue, hypoglycemia and yeast infections all drain the body's energy reserve and leave it in a weakened state. By drinking a glass of tomato juice with a pinch of cayenne pepper and a dash of hot sauce, well stirred, the liver and adrenal glands will become revitalized within 30 minutes.

• Graham A. Colditz M.D. and his associates at Howard Medical School interviewed more than 1000 people about their diets and then tracked their health for 5 years. They found that the chances of dying of cancer were lowest among those who ate tomatoes and strawberries every week. Tomatoes are rich in vitamins A and C, low in fat and sodium, contain some fiber and are rich in potassium.

Food Combining

• As stated in *The Food Combining Bible*, tomatoes combine with mushrooms, vegetables, avocados, oil and protein.

Kitchen Tips

• For the finest flavor, keep fresh tomatoes at room temperature. They ripen at temperatures between 50° and 85°. Keep them out, or they lose flavor. To freeze fresh tomatoes, blanch them in boiling water for about two minutes, then plunge them quickly into ice water and drain. Remove skin or chop and freeze in recipe-sized portions for up to 1 year.

Tomato Soup with Zucchini Chips Recipe

INGREDIENTS:

2 large cans of crushed tomatoes
1 large can of tomato puree
1 large can of diced tomatoes
3 cloves of pressed or minced garlic
3 T paprika
2 T vegetable broth
1 diced red pepper (optional)
1 diced zucchini
1 diced onion
liquid amino to taste

DIRECTIONS:

Sauté garlic and vegetables in a pan with paprika. Add tomato puree, diced tomatoes, and vegetable broth and then bring to a simmer. Add liquid amino to taste.

ZUCCHINI CHIPS:

INGREDIENTS:

3 sliced zucchinis
3 tablespoons of liquid amino
1/4 cup rice parmesan cheese or nutritional yeast
1/2 cup lemon juice

DIRECTIONS:

Slice zucchini into slices 1/4-inch thick. Soak them in lemon juice and liquid amino for 10 minutes. Then place in the oven on warm to dehydrate until they are of chip consistency (approximately 10 hours), or you may cook them at a higher temperature, checking often for chip crispiness. These chips are excellent with soup.

BLOOD TYPE GROUPS:
AB   O

Red Hot Coolers Recipe

INGREDIENTS:

32 ounces fresh squeezed or jar of tomato juice

4 sticks of celery

Juice of 2 limes

3 T of celery seed

4 ounces of vegetarian Worcestershire sauce (or to taste)

Tabasco to taste

Spike (one shake)

1 slice of lemon

DIRECTIONS:

Wet the rim of a glass with the juice of the lime, then turn the glass upside down, placing the rim into a saucer containing the celery seed, seasoning the rim of the glass. Inside of the glass, mix tomato juice, 1 ounce of Worcestershire sauce, the juice of half of a lime, tabasco sauce to taste and one stick of celery. Place the slice of lemon on the rim of the glass and serve.

BLOOD TYPE GROUPS:

AB   O

Beneficial and Neutral Foods for all Blood Types

FISH

Cod, Croaker, Drum, Mackerel, Mahi-mahi, Orange Roughy, Parrotfish, Ocean Perch, Silver Perch, White Perch, Yellow Perch, Pickerel, Pike, Porgy, Red Snapper, Salmon, Sardine, Smelt, Tilapia, Tuna, Whitefish

DAIRY

Feta Cheese, Ghee, Goat Cheese

EGG

Chicken: egg, egg white and egg yolk

BEAN/LEGUME

Cannellini Bean, Green/ Snap/String Bean, Jicama, Northern Bean, Snap Bean, White Bean

NUT/SEED

Almond/Almond Butter, Almond Cheese, Almond Milk, Flaxseed (Linseed)

GRAIN

Essene Bread (Manna Bread), Ezekiel Bread, Gluten-free Bread, Millet, Quinoa, Cream of Rice, Puffed Rice, Rice (White/ Brown/Basmati) Bread, Rice Bran, Rice Cake/ Flour, Rice Milk, Spelt (Whole), Spelt Flour/ Products

VEGETABLE/ VEG JUICE

Agar, Arugula, Asparagus, Asparagus Pea, Bamboo Shoot, Beet, Beet Greens, Bok Choy, Broccoli, Brussels Sprouts, Cabbage Juice, Carrot, Carrot Juice, Celeriac, Celery/Celery Juice, Chicory, Daikon Radish, Dandelion, Endive, Escarole, Fennel, Fiddlehead Fern, Garlic, Ginger, Horseradish, Kelp, Kohlrabi, All Lettuce, Portobello Mushroom, Okra, Onion (Red/ Yellow/White/Green/ Spanish), Parsnip, Pea (Green/Pod/Snow), Pimento, Radicchio, Rappini, Rutabaga, Scallion, Seaweed, Shallot, Spinach/Spinach Juice, Squash (Summer/ Winter), Turnip, Water Chestnut, Watercress, Zucchini

FRUIT/ FRUIT JUICE

Apple/Apple Juice/Cider, Apricot/Apricot Juice, Blueberry, Boysenberry, Breadfruit, Canag Melon, Casaba Melon, All Cherries, Black Cherry Juice, Christmas Melon, Cranberry, Cranberry Juice, Crenshaw Melon, Currants (Black/Red), All Dates, Elderberry Dark/ Blue/Purple), Fig (Fresh/ Dried), Gooseberry, All Grapes, Grapefruit, Grapefruit Juice, Kumquat, Lemon/Lemon Juice, Lime/Lime Juice, Loganberry, Mulberry, Muskmelon, Nectarine/ Nectarine Juice, Peach, Pear/Pear Juice, Persian Melon, Pineapple, Pineapple Juice, Plum (Dark/Green/Red), Prune, Raisin, Raspberry, Spanish Melon, Strawberry, Water and Lemon, Watermelon, Youngberry

OIL

Almond Oil, Black Currant Seed Oil, Cod Liver Oil, Flaxseed (Linseed) Oil, Olive Oil

HERB/SPICE

Arrowroot, Basil, Bay Leaf, Bergamot, Caraway, Cardamom, Carob, Chervil, Chives, Chocolate, Cilantro, Clove, Coriander, Cream of Tartar, Cumin, Curry, Dill, Dulse, Licorice Root, Marjoram, Dry Mustard, Oregano, Parsley, Paprika, Peppermint, Rosemary, Saffron, Sage, Savory, Senna, Spearmint, Tarragon, Thyme, Turmeric, Vanilla

CONDIMENT

Apple Pectin, Jam/Jelly (with right ingredients), Mustard (wheat-free and vinegar-free), Salad Dressing (with right ingredients), Sea Salt, Tamari (wheat-free), Baker's Yeast, Brewer's Yeast

SWEETENER

Honey, Maple Syrup, Molasses, Blackstrap Molasses, Rice Syrup, Sugar (Brown/White)

BEVERAGE

Green Tea

Blood Group A

FISH

BENEFICIAL

Cod, Mackerel, Silver Perch, Yellow Perch, Pickerel, Pollack, Red Snapper, Salmon, Sardine, Rainbow Trout, Sea Trout, Whitefish, Whiting

NEUTRAL

Sea Bass, Butterfish, Croaker, Drum, Mahi-mahi, Orange Roughy, Parrotfish, Porgy, Ocean Perch, White Perch, Pike, Salmon Roe, Smelt, Tilapia, Brook Trout, Tuna, Yellowtail

AVOID

Anchovy, Bluegill Bass, Striped Bass, Bluefish, Flounder, Gray Sole, Grouper, Haddock, Hake, Halibut, Herring, Lox (Smoked Salmon), Shad, Sole, Tilefish

DAIRY

BENEFICIAL

None

NEUTRAL

Feta Cheese, Ghee, Goat Cheese, Goat Milk, Yogurt

AVOID

Butter, Casein, Cottage Cheese, Whey and all others conflict with perfect health.

EGG

BENEFICIAL

None

NEUTRAL

Chicken: egg, egg white and egg yolk

AVOID

All others conflict with perfect health.

BEAN/LEGUME

BENEFICIAL

Adzuki Bean, Black Bean, Green/Snap/String Bean, Domestic Lentil, Green Lentil, Red Lentil

NEUTRAL

Cannellini Bean, Jicama, Mung Bean Sprouts, Northern Bean, Snap Bean, White Bean

AVOID

Copper Bean, Garbanzo (Chickpea) Bean, Navy Bean, Red Bean

NUT/SEED

BENEFICIAL

Flaxseed (Linseed), Pumpkin Seed/Pumpkin Seed Butter

NEUTRAL

Almond/Almond Butter, Almond Cheese, Almond Milk, Poppy Seed, Sesame Seed, Sesame Butter/ Tahini, Sunflower Seed, Sunflower Seed Butter

AVOID

All others conflict with perfect health.

GRAIN

BENEFICIAL

Amaranth, Artichoke Flour/Pasta, Essene Bread, Ezekiel Bread, Rye Flour (Whole Rye), Rye/100 percent Rye Bread

NEUTRAL

Barley, Gluten-free bread, Millet, Quinoa, Cream of Rice, Puffed Rice, Rice (White/Brown/Basmati) Bread, Wild Rice, Rice Bran, Rice Cake/Flour, Rice Milk, Sorghum, Whole Spelt, Spelt Flour/ Products, Tapioca

AVOID

All others conflict with perfect health.

VEGETABLE/ VEG JUICE

BENEFICIAL

Alfalfa Sprouts, Aloe/Aloe Tea/Aloe Juice, Artichoke (Globe/Jerusalem), Beet Greens, Broccoli, Carrot, Carrot Juice, Celery/ Celery Juice, Chicory, Dandelion, Escarole, Fennel, Garlic, Ginger, Horseradish, Kohlrabi, Leek, Romaine Lettuce, Okra, Onion (Red/ Spanish/Yellow/White/ Green), Parsnip, Rappini, Spinach/Spinach Juice, Turnip

NEUTRAL

Agar, Arugula, Asparagus, Asparagus Pea, Bamboo Shoot, Beet, Bok Choy, Brussel Sprouts, Cabbage Juice, Cauliflower, Celeriac, Cucumber Juice, Daikon Radish, Endive, Fiddlehead Fern, Kelp, Lettuce (except Romaine), Portabella Mushroom, Mustard Greens, Green Olives, Pimento, Raddichio, Radish, Radish Sprouts, Rutabaga, Scallion, Seaweed, Shallot, Squash (Summer/Winter), Taro, Water Chestnut, Watercress, Zucchini

VEGETABLE/ VEG JUICE

(CONT'D)

AVOID

Cabbage (Chinese/Red/ White), Caper, Chili Pepper, Eggplant, Juniper, Shiitake Mushroom, Olive (Black/Greek/Spanish), Pea (Green/Pod/Snow), Pepper (Green/Jalapeño/ Red/Yellow/Cayenne), Potato (White/Red/ Blue/ Yellow), Rhubarb, Sauerkraut, Tomato/ Tomato Juice, Yucca

FRUIT/ FRUIT JUICE

BENEFICIAL

Apricot/Apricot Juice, Blackberry/Blackberry Juice, Blueberry, Boysenberry, Cherry (ALL), Black Cherry Juice, Cranberry, Fig (Fresh/ Dried), Grapefruit, Grapefruit Juice, Lime/ Lime Juice, Lemon/Lemon Juice, Pineapple/Pineapple Juice, Plum (Dark/Green/ Red), Prune, Water and Lemon

NEUTRAL

Apple/Apple Juice/Cider, Asian Pear, Avocado, Breadfruit, Canag Melon, Cantaloupe, Casaba Melon, Christmas Melon, Cranberry Juice, Crenshaw Melon, Currants (Black/Red),

Dates (ALL), Dewberry, Elderberry (Dark/Blue/ Purple), Gooseberry, Grapes (ALL), Guava/ Guava Juice, Kiwi, Kumquat, Loganberry, Mulberry, Muskmelon, Nectarine/Nectarine Juice, Peach, Pear/Pear Juice, Persian Melon, Persimmon, Pomegranate, Prickly Pear, Quince, Raisin, Raspberry, Sago Palm, Spanish Melon, Starfruit (Carambola), Strawberry, Watermelon, Youngberry

AVOID

Banana, Bitter Melon, Coconut, Coconut Milk, Honeydew Melon, Mango/Mango Juice, Orange/Orange Juice, Papaya/Papaya Juice, Plantain, Tangerine

OIL

BENEFICIAL

Black Currant Seed Oil, Flaxseed (Linseed) Oil, Olive Oil

NEUTRAL

Almond Oil, Borage Seed Oil, Cod Liver Oil, Evening Primrose Oil, Sesame Oil, Safflower Oil, Sunflower Oil

AVOID

Castor Oil, Coconut Oil

HERB/SPICE

BENEFICIAL

Dry Mustard, Parsley, Turmeric

NEUTRAL

Allspice, Anise, Arrowroot, Basil, Bay Leaf, Bergamot, Caraway, Cardamom, Carob, Chervil, Chives, Chocolate, Cilantro, Cinnamon, Clove, Coriander, Cream of Tartar, Cumin, Curry, Dill, Dulse, Guarana, Licorice Root, Mace, Marjoram, Nutmeg, Oregano, Paprika, Peppermint, Rosemary, Saffron, Sage, Savory, Senna, Spearmint, Tarragon, Thyme, Vanilla

AVOID

Acacia (Arabic Gum), Chili Powder, Pepper (Black/White/ Peppercorn/Red Flakes), Wintergreen

CONDIMENT

BENEFICIAL

Tamari (Wheat-free), Mustard (wheat-free, vin-egar-free)

NEUTRAL

Apple Pectin, Jam/Jelly (with right ingredients), Mustard (with vinegar, wheat-free), Sea Salt, Brewer's Yeast, Baker's Yeast

AVOID

Carrageenan, Guar Gum, Ketchup, Mayonnaise, Mustard (with vinegar and wheat), Pickle Relish, Apple Cider Vinegar, Vinegar (Balsamic/ White/Red/Rice), Worcestershire Sauce

SWEETENER

BENEFICIAL

Barley Malt, Blackstrap Molasses

NEUTRAL

Almond Extract, Dextrose, Fructose, Honey, Invert Sugar, Maltodextrin, Maple Syrup, Molasses, Rice Syrup, Stevia, Sugar (Brown/White)

AVOID

Sucanat and all others conflict with perfect health.

BEVERAGE

BENEFICIAL

Green Tea

NEUTRAL

None

AVOID

Tea (Black Regular/ Decaf) and all others conflict with perfect health.

Blood Group AB

FISH

BENEFICIAL

Cod, Grouper, Mackerel, Mahi-mahi, Pickerel, Pike, Porgy, Red Snapper, Salmon, Sardine, Shad, Tuna

NEUTRAL

Bluefish, Butterfish, Croaker, Drum, Herring, Orange Roughy, Parrotfish, Ocean Perch, Silver Perch, White Perch, Yellow Perch, Pollack, Smelt, Tilapia, Tilefish, Whitefish

AVOID

Anchovy, Bluegill Bass, Sea Bass, Striped Bass, Flounder, Gray Sole, Haddock, Hake, Halibut, Salmon Roe, Sole, Brook Trout, Rainbow Trout, Sea Trout, Whiting, Yellowtail

DAIRY

BENEFICIAL

Cottage Cheese, Feta Cheese, Goat Cheese, Goat Milk, Yogurt

NEUTRAL

Casein, Whey, Ghee

AVOID

Butter

EGG

BENEFICIAL

Chicken: egg white

NEUTRAL

Chicken: egg and egg yolk

AVOID

All others conflict with perfect health.

BEAN/LEGUME

BENEFICIAL

Green Lentil and Navy Bean

NEUTRAL

Cannelini Bean, Copper Bean, Green/Snap/String/ Bean, Jicama, Domestic Lentil, Red Lentil, Northern Bean, Snap Bean, White Bean

AVOID

Adzuki Bean, Black Bean, Garbanzo (Chickpea) Bean, Mung Bean Sprouts

NUT/SEED

BENEFICIAL

None

NEUTRAL

Almond/Almond Butter, Almond Cheese, Almond Milk, Flaxseed (Linseed)

AVOID

Pumpkin Seed/Pumpkin Seed Butter, Sesame Butter/Tahini, Sesame Seed, Sunflower Seed/ Sunflower Seed Butter

GRAIN

BENEFICIAL

Amaranth, Essene Bread (Manna Bread), Ezekiel Bread, Millet, Puffed Rice, Rice (White/Brown/ Basmati) Bread, Rice Bran, Rice Cake/Flour, Rice Milk, Whole Spelt, Wild Rice

NEUTRAL

Barley, Gluten-free Bread, Quinoa, Cream of Rice, Spelt Flour/ Products

AVOID

Artichoke Flour/Pasta, Sorghum, Tapioca

VEGETABLE/ VEG JUICE

BENEFICIAL

Alfalfa Sprouts, Beet, Beet Greens, Broccoli, Cabbage Juice, Carrot Juice, Cauliflower, Celery/ Celery Juice, Dandelion, Eggplant, Garlic, Mustard Greens, Parsnip

NEUTRAL

Agar, Arugula, Asparagus, Asparagus Pea, Bamboo Shoot Bok Choy, Brussel Sprouts, Cabbage (Chinese/Red/White), Carrot, Celeriac, Chicory, Cucumber Juice, Daikon Radish, Endive, Escarole, Fennel, Fiddlehead Fern, Ginger, Horseradish, Juniper, Kelp, Kohlrabi, Leek, Lettuce (including Romaine), Portabella Mushroom, Okra, Olive(Greek/Spanish/ Green), Onion(Red/ Spanish/Yellow/White/ Green), Pea (Green/ Pod/ Snow), Pimento, Potato (White/Red/ Blue/ Yellow), Radicchio, Rappini, Rutabaga, Sauerkraut, Scallion, Seaweed, Shallot, Spinach/ Spinach Juice, Squash (Summer/Winter), Tomato/Tomato Juice, Turnip, Water Chestnut, Watercress, Yucca, Zucchini

AVOID

Aloe/Aloe Tea/Aloe Juice, Artichoke (Globe/ Jerusalem), Caper, Chili Pepper, Shiitake Mushroom, Olive (Black), Pepper (Green/Yellow/ Jalapeño/Red/Cayenne), Pickle in vinegar, Radish, Radish Sprouts, Rhubarb

FRUIT/ FRUIT JUICE

BENEFICIAL

Cherry (ALL), Cherry Juice (Black), Cranberry/ Cranberry Juice, Fig (Fresh/ Dried), Gooseberry, Grape (ALL), Grapefruit, Kiwi, Lemon/Lemon Juice, Loganberry, Pineapple, Plum (Dark/Green/Red), Watermelon

NEUTRAL

Apple/Apple Juice/Cider, Apricot/Apricot Juice, Asian Pear, Blackberry/ Blackberry Juice, Blueberry, Boysenberry, Breadfruit, Canag Melon, Cantaloupe, Casaba Melon, Christmas Melon, Crenshaw Melon, Currants (Red/Black), Date (ALL), Elderberry (Dark/Blue/Purple), Grapefruit Juice, Honeydew, Kumquat, Lime/ Lime Juice, Mulberry, Muskmelon, Nectarine/ Nectarine Juice, Papaya/ Papaya Juice, Peach, Pear/ Pear Juice, Persian Melon, Pineapple Juice, Plantain, Prune, Raisin, Raspberry, Spanish Melon, Strawberry, Tangerine, Water and Lemon, Youngberry

AVOID

Avocado, Banana, Bitter Melon, Coconut, Coconut Milk, Dewberry, Guava/Guava Juice, Mango/Mango Juice, Orange/Orange Juice, Persimmon, Pomegranate, Prickly Pear, Quince, Sago Palm, Starfruit (Carambola)

OIL

BENEFICIAL

Olive Oil

NEUTRAL

Almond Oil, Black Currant Seed Oil, Borage Seed Oil, Castor Oil, Cod Liver Oil, Flaxseed (Linseed) Oil

AVOID

Coconut Oil, Safflower Oil, Sesame Oil, Sunflower Oil

HERB/SPICE

BENEFICIAL

Parsley and Curry

NEUTRAL

Arrowroot, Basil, Bay Leaf, Bergamot, Caraway, Cardamom, Carob, Chervil, Chili Powder, Chives, Chocolate, Cilantro, Cinnamon, Clove, Coriander, Cream of Tartar, Cumin, Dill, Dulse, Licorice Root, Mace, Marjoram, Dry Mustard, Nutmeg, Paprika, Peppermint, Rosemary, Saffron, Sage, Savory, Senna, Spearmint, Tarragon, Thyme, Turmeric, Vanilla, Wintergreen

AVOID

Acacia (Arabic Gum), Allspice, Anise, Guarana, Pepper(Black/White/ Peppercorn/Red Flakes)

CONDIMENT

Beneficial

None

NEUTRAL

Apple Pectin, Jam/Jelly (with right ingredients), Mustard (wheat-free, vinegar-free), Salad Dressing (with right ingredients), Sea Salt, Tamari (wheat-free), Baker's Yeast, Brewer's Yeast

AVOID

Carrageenan, Guar Gum, Ketchup, Mustard (with vinegar and wheat), Mustard (with vinegar and wheat-free), Pickle Relish, Apple Cider Vinegar, Vinegar (Balsamic/White/Red/ Rice), Worcestershire Sauce

SWEETENER

BENEFICIAL

Blackstrap Molasses

NEUTRAL

Honey, Maple Syrup, Molasses, Rice Syrup, Stevia, Sugar (Brown/ White)

AVOID

Almond Extract, Barley Malt, Dextrose, Fructose, Invert Sugar, Maltodextrin, Sucanat

BEVERAGE

BENEFICIAL

Green Tea

NEUTRAL

None

AVOID

Tea (Black Regular/ Decaf)

FISH

BENEFICIAL

Cod, Croaker, Flounder, Grouper, Haddock, Hake, Halibut, Mackerel, Mahi-mahi, Ocean Perch, Pickerel, Pike, Porgy, Salmon, Sardine, Shad, Sole

NEUTRAL

Bluefish, Drum, Gray Sole, Herring, Orange Roughy, Parrotfish, Silver Perch, White Perch, Yellow Perch, Red Snapper, Smelt, Tilapia, Tilefish, Tuna, Whitefish, Whiting

AVOID

Anchovy, Bluegill Bass, Lox (Smoked Salmon), Sea Bass, Striped Bass, Butterfish, Pollack, Salmon Roe, Brook Trout, Rainbow Trout, Sea Trout, Yellowtail

DAIRY

BENEFICIAL

Cottage Cheese, Feta Cheese, Goat Cheese, Goat Milk, Yogurt

NEUTRAL

Butter, Casein, Ghee, Whey

AVOID

All others conflict with perfect health.

EGG

BENEFICIAL

None

NEUTRAL

Chicken: egg, egg white, and egg yolk

AVOID

All others conflict with perfect health.

BEAN/LEGUME

BENEFICIAL

Navy Bean

NEUTRAL

Cannellini Bean, Copper Bean, Green/Snap/String Bean, Jicama, Northern Bean, White Bean

AVOID

Adzuki, Black, Garbanzo (Chickpea), Domestic Lentil, Green Lentil, Red Lentil, Mung Bean Sprouts

NUT/SEED

BENEFICIAL

None

NEUTRAL

Almond/Almond Butter, Almond Cheese, Almond Milk, Flaxseed (Linseed)

AVOID

Poppy Seed, Pumpkin Seed/Pumpkin Seed Butter, Sesame Seed, Sesame Butter/Tahini, Sunflower Seed/ Sunflower Seed Butter

GRAIN

BENEFICIAL

Essene Bread (Manna Bread), Ezekiel Bread, Millet, Puffed Rice, Rice Bran, Rice Cake/Flour, Rice Milk, Whole Spelt

NEUTRAL

Barley, Gluten-free Bread, Quinoa, Cream of Rice, Rice (White/Brown/ Basmati) Bread, Spelt Flour Products

AVOID

Amaranth, Artichoke Flour/Pasta, Wild Rice, Rye Flour, Rye/100% Rye Bread, Sorghum, Tapioca

VEGETABLE/ VEG. JUICE

BENEFICIAL

Beet, Beet Greens, Broccoli, Brussel Sprouts, Cabbage (Chinese/Red/ White), Cabbage Juice, Carrot, Cauliflower, Eggplant, Ginger, Shiitake Mushroom, Mustard Greens, Parsnip, Pepper (Green/Yellow/Jalapeño/ Red/Cayenne)

NEUTRAL

Agar, Alfalfa Sprouts, Arugula, Asparagus, Asparagus Pea, Bamboo Shoot, Bok Choy, Caper, Carrot Juice, Celeriac, Celery/Celery Juice, Chicory, Chili Pepper, Cucumber Juice, Daikon Radish, Dandelion, Endive, Escarole, Fennel, Fiddlehead Fern, Garlic, Horseradish, Kelp, Kohlrabi, Leek, Lettuce (including Romaine, Portabella Mushroom, Okra, Onion (Red/Spanish/Yellow/ White/Green), Pea (Green/Pod/Snow), Pickle in vinegar, Pimento, Potato (White/Red/ Blue/ Yellow), Radicchio, Rappini, Rutabaga, Sauerkraut, Scallion, Seaweed, Shallot, Spinach/ Spinach Juice, Squash (Summer/White), Taro, Turnip, Water Chestnut, Watercress, Yucca, Zucchini

AVOID

Aloe/Aloe Tea/Aloe Juice, Artichoke (Globe/ Jerusalem), Juniper, Olives (Greek/ Spanish/ Black/Green), Radish, Radish Sprouts, Rhubarb, Tomato/Tomato Juice

Blood Group B (Continued)

FRUIT/ FRUIT JUICE

BENEFICIAL

Banana, Cranberry/ Cranberry Juice, Grape (ALL), Papaya/Papaya Juice, Pineapple/ Pineapple Juice, Plum (Dark/Green/Red), Watermelon, Youngberry

NEUTRAL

Apple/Apple Juice/ Cider, Apricot/Apricot Juice, Asian Pear, Blackberry/ Blackberry Juice, Blueberry Juice, Boysenberry, Breadfruit, Canag Melon, Cantaloupe, Casaba Melon, Cherry (ALL), Cherry Juice (Black), Christmas Melon, Crenshaw Melon, Currants (Black/Red), Date (ALL), Dewberry, Elderberry (Dark/Blue/ Purple), Fig (Fresh/ Dried), Gooseberry, Grapefruit/Grapefruit Juice, Guava/Guava Juice, Honeydew, Kiwi, Kumquat, Lemon/Lemon Juice, Lime/Lime Juice, Loganberry, Mango/ Mango Juice, Mulberry, Muskmelon, Nectarine/ Nectarine Juice, Orange/ Orange Juice, Peach, Pear/Pear Juice, Persian Melon, Plantain, Prune, Quince, Raisin, Raspberry, Sago Palm, Spanish Melon, Strawberry, Tangerine, Water and Lemon

AVOID

Avocado, Bitter Melon, Coconut/Coconut Milk, Persimmon, Pomegranate, Prickly Pear, Starfruit (Carambola)

OIL

BENEFICIAL

Olive Oil

NEUTRAL

Almond Oil, Black Currant Seed Oil, Cod Liver Oil, Evening Primrose Oil, Flaxseed (Linseed) Oil

AVOID

Borage Seed Oil, Castor Oil, Safflower Oil, Sesame Oil, Sunflower Oil

HERB/SPICE

BENEFICIAL

Curry, Licorice Root, Parsley

NEUTRAL

Anise, Arrowroot, Basil, Bay Leaf, Bergamot, Caraway, Cardamom, Carob, Chervil, Chili Powder, Chives, Chocolate, Cilantro, Clove, Coriander, Cream of Tartar, Cumin, Dill, Dulse, Mace, Marjoram, Dry Mustard, Nutmeg, Oregano, Paprika, Pepper (Peppercorn/Red Flakes), Peppermint, Rosemary, Saffron, Sage, Savory, Senna, Spearmint, Tarragon, Thyme, Turmeric, Vanilla, Wintergreen

AVOID

Acacia (Arabic Gum), Allspice, Cinnamon, Guarana, Pepper (Black/ White)

CONDIMENT

BENEFICIAL

None

NEUTRAL

Apple Pectin, Jam/Jelly (with right ingredients), Mayonnaise, Mustard, Pickle Relish, Salad Dressing (with right ingredients), Sea Salt, Tamari (wheat-free), Apple Cider Vinegar, Vinegar (Balsamic/ White/ Red/Rice), Baker's Yeast, Brewer's Yeast

AVOID

Carrageenan, Guar Gum, Ketchup, Worcestershire Sauce

SWEETENER

BENEFICIAL

Blackstrap Molasses

NEUTRAL

Fructose, Honey, Maple Syrup, Molasses, Rice Syrup, Sugar (Brown/ White)

AVOID

Almond Extract, Barley Malt, Dextrose, Invert Sugar, Maltodextrin, Stevia, Sucanat

BEVERAGE

BENEFICIAL

Green Tea

NEUTRAL

Tea (Black Regular/ Decaf)

AVOID

All others conflict with perfect health.

Blood Group O

FISH

BENEFICIAL

Bluegill Bass, Sea Bass, Striped Bass, Cod, Halibut, Ocean Perch, Silver Perch, White Perch, Yellow Perch, Pike, Red Snapper, Shad, Sole, Tilefish, Rainbow Trout, Yellowtail

NEUTRAL

Anchovy, Bluefish, Butterfish, Croaker, Drum, Flounder, Gray Sole, Grouper, Haddock, Hake, Herring, Mackerel, Mahi-mahi, Orange Roughy, Parrotfish, Pickerel, Porgy, Salmon, Sardine, Smelt, Tilapia, Brook Trout, Sea Trout, Tuna, Whitefish, Whiting

AVOID

Pollack, Salmon Roe

DAIRY

BENEFICIAL

None

NEUTRAL

Butter, Feta Cheese, Ghee, Goat Cheese

AVOID

Casein, Cottage Cheese, Whey, Yogurt and all others conflict with perfect health.

EGG

BENEFICIAL

None

NEUTRAL

Chicken:egg, egg white and egg yolk

AVOID

All others conflict with perfect health.

BEAN/ LEGUME

BENEFICIAL

Adzuki Bean

NEUTRAL

Black Bean, Cannellini, Garbanzo Bean (Chickpea), Green/Snap/ String Bean, Jicama, Mung Bean Sprouts, Northern Bean, Snap Bean, White Bean

AVOID

Copper Bean, Domestic Lentil, Green Lentil, Red Lentil, Navy Bean

NUT/ SEED

BENEFICIAL

Flaxseed (Linseed), Pumpkin Seed/Pumpkin Seed Butter

NEUTRAL

Almond/Almond Butter, Almond Cheese, Almond Milk, Sesame Butter/ Tahini, Sesame Seed

AVOID

Poppy Seed, Sunflower Seed/Sunflower Seed Butter

GRAIN

BENEFICIAL

Essence Bread

NEUTRAL

Amaranth, Artichoke Flour/ Pasta, Ezekiel Bread, Gluten-free Bread, Millet, Quinoa, Cream of Rice, Puffed Rice, Rice (White/ Brown/Basmati) Bread, Wild Rice, Rice Bran, Rice Cake/Flour, Rice Milk, Whole Spelt, Spelt Flour/Products, Tapioca

AVOID

Barley and Sorghum

VEGETABLE/ VEG. JUICE

BENEFICIAL

Artichoke (Globe/ Jerusalem), Beet Greens, Broccoli, Chicory, Dandelion, Escarole, Ginger, Horseradish, Kelp, Kohlrabi, Romaine Lettuce, Okra, Onion (Red/Spanish/Yellow/ White/Green), Parsnip, Pepper (Red/Cayenne), Seaweed, Spinach/ Spinach Juice, Swiss Chard, Turnip

NEUTRAL

Agar, Arugula, Asparagus, Asparagus Pea, Bamboo Shoot, Beet, Bok Choy, Brussel Sprouts, Cabbage (Chinese/Red/White), Cabbage Juice, Carrot, Carrot Juice, Celeriac, Celery/Celery Juice, Chili Pepper, Daikon Radish, Eggplant, Endive, Fennel, Fiddlehead Fern, Garlic, Lettuce (except Romaine), Portabella Mushroom, Olive (Greek/Spanish/Green), Pea (Green/Pod/Snow), Pepper (Green/Yellow/ Jalapeño), Pimento, Radicchio, Rappini, Radish, Radish Sprouts, Rutabaga, Sauerkraut, Scallion, Shallot, Squash (Summer/Winter), Taro, Tomato/ Tomato Juice, Water Chestnut, Watercress, Zucchini

AVOID

Alfalfa Sprouts, Aloe/ Aloe Tea/Aloe Juice

VEGETABLE/ VEG JUICE (CONT'D)

AVOID

Caper, Cauliflower, Juniper, Leek, Shiitake Mushroom, Mustard Greens, Black Olives, Pickles, Potato (White/ Red/Blue/Yellow), Rhubarb, Yucca

FRUIT/ FRUIT JUICE

BENEFICIAL

Banana, Blueberry, Cherry (ALL), Cherry Juice (Black), Fig (Fresh/ Dried), Guava/Guava Juice, Mango/Mango Juice, Pineapple Juice, Plum (Dark/Green/Red), Prune

NEUTRAL

Apple/Apple Juice/ Cider, Apricot Juice, Boysenberry, Breadfruit, Canag Melon, Cantaloupe, Casaba Melon, Christmas Melon, Cranberry/Cranberry Juice, Crenshaw Melon, Currants (Black/Red), Date (ALL), Dewberry, Elderberry (Dark/Blue/ Purple), Gooseberry, Grape (ALL), Grapefruit/ Grapefruit Juice, Kumquat, Lemon/Lemon Juice, Lime/ Lime Juice, Loganberry, Mulberry,

Muskmelon, Nectarine/ Nectarine Juice, Papaya/ Papaya Juice, Peach, Pear/ Pear Juice, Persian Melon, Persimmon, Pineapple, Pomegranate, Prickly Pear, Quince, Raisin, Raspberry, Sago Palm, Spanish Melon, Starfruit (Carambola), Strawberry, Water and Lemon, Watermelon, Youngberry

AVOID

Asian Pear, Avocado, Bitter Melon, Blackberry/ Blackberry Juice, Cantaloupe, Coconut, Coconut Milk, Honeydew Melon, Kiwi, Orange/ Orange Juice, Plantain, Tangerine

OIL

BENEFICIAL

Flaxseed (Linseed) Oil, Olive Oil

NEUTRAL

Almond Oil, Black Currant Seed Oil, Borage Seed Oil, Cod Liver Oil, Sesame Oil

AVOID

Castor Oil, Coconut Oil, Evening Primrose Oil, Sunflower Oil

HERB/ SPICE

BENEFICIAL

Carob, Curry, Dulse, Parsley, Turmeric

NEUTRAL

Allspice, Anise, Arrowroot, Basil, Bay Leaf, Bergamot, Caraway, Cardamom, Chervil, Chili Powder, Chives, Chocolate, Cilantro, Cinnamon, Clove, Coriander, Cream of Tartar, Cumin, Dill, Licorice Root, Marjoram, Dry Mustard, Oregano, Paprika, Pepper (Peppercorn/ Red Flakes), Peppermint, Rosemary, Saffron, Sage, Savory, Senna, Spearmint, Tarragon, Thyme, Vanilla, Wintergreen

AVOID

Acacia (Arabic Gum), Guarana, Mace, Nutmeg, Pepper (Black/White)

CONDIMENT

BENEFICIAL

None

NEUTRAL

Apple Pectin, Jam/Jelly (with right ingredients), Mustard (vinegar-free, wheat-free), Salad Dressing (with right ingredients), Sea Salt, Tamari (wheat-free), Apple Cider

Vinegar, Baker's Yeast, Brewer's Yeast

AVOID

Carrageenan, Guar Gum, Ketchup, Mustard (with vinegar and/or wheat), Pickle Relish, Vinegar (Balsamic/White/Red/ Rice), Worcestershire Sauce

SWEETENER

BENEFICIAL

None

NEUTRAL

Almond Extract, Barley Malt, Honey, Maple Syrup, Molasses, Blackstrap Molasses, Rice Syrup, Stevia, Sucanat, Sugar (Brown/White)

AVOID

Dextrose, Fructose, Invert Sugar, Maltodextrin

BEVERAGE

BENEFICIAL

Green Tea

NEUTRAL

None

AVOID

Tea (Black Regular/ Decaf)

Cooking Tips

READ THE INGREDIENTS when purchasing food items. You may not be getting what you think you are purchasing.

Avoid vegetable oil. Ninety-nine percent of all vegetable oil is soybean oil. Both soybean oil and canola oil congest the cells and have a high viscosity rate, which means they don't break down. Canola has the viscosity of motor oil.

Instead of sautéing in oil, add small amounts of hot water to keep vegetables from sticking. A little olive oil can be added after cooking; this keeps the oil from going rancid from overheating. Olive oil is the best oil for human consumption; however, it is not as heat tolerant as other oils.

A cooking stone can be used to add minerals to soups or beans just as a cast iron pan adds iron to food. Simply add it to the pot at the start of the preparation.

Spinach should be eaten raw or wilted (by pouring hot water or placing over steam). Cooked spinach contains oxalate acid, which produces kidney stones—if eaten consistently.

When baking in the oven, the top rack is used for browning the top of the item, thus rotating items while baking allows for even cooking.

It's best to use fresh herbs to season. Too much seasoning impedes and digestion tends to make facial skin look aged.

Beans should be soaked overnight. To degas beans, rinse thoroughly with 1 tablespoon of baking soda. You can also bring beans to a rolling boil, and be sure to remove foam frequently.

Vinegar and lemon juice are excellent substitutes for salt. They both enhance flavor and have a saline undertone.

Selected Bibliography

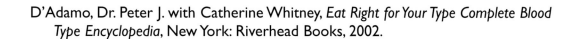

D'Adamo, Dr. Peter J. with Catherine Whitney, *Eat Right for Your Type Complete Blood Type Encyclopedia*, New York: Riverhead Books, 2002.

Dollemore, Doug, Mark Giuliucci, Jennifer Haigh, Sid Kirchheimer, and Jean Callahan, *New Choices in Natural Healing: Over 1,800 of the Best Self-Help Remedies from the World of Alternative Medicine*, New York: Rodale Books, 1995.

Dries, Jan and Inge Dries, *The Food Combining Bible*, London: Element Books, 2002.

Duke, James A., Ph.D., *The Green Pharmacy: The Ultimate Compendium of Natural Remedies from the World's Foremost Authority on Healing Herbs*, New York: St. Martin's Paperbacks, 1997.

Green, Aliza, *The Bean Bible: A Legumaniac's Guide to Lentils, Peas, and Every Edible Bean on the Planet!,* Philadelphia: Running Press Book Publishers, 2000.

Hausman, Patricia and Judith Benn Hurley, *The Healing Foods, The Ultimate Authority on the Curative Power of Nutrition*, New York: Dell Books, 1989.

Heinerman, John, *Heinerman's Encyclopedia of Healing Juices*, Upper Saddle River, N.J.: Prentice Hall Press, 1994.

Kornfeld, Myra and George Minot, *The Voluptuous Vegan*, New York: Clarkson Potter, 2000.

Meyerowitz, Steve, et. al., *Sproutman's Kitchen Garden Cookbook: 250 Flourless, Dairyless, Low Temperature, Low Fat, Low Salt, Living Food Vegetarian Recipes*, Great Barrington, Massachusetts: Sproutman Publications, 1999.

Shannon, Nomi, *The Raw Gourmet*, Vancouver, Canada: Alive Books, 1999.

Index